THE
AI PLAYBOOK
FOR SMBs

FROM AI RISK TO ADOPTION FOR BUSINESS LEADERS

ART GROSS

Contents

APPENDICES

INTRODUCTION

WHY THIS BOOK IS FOR YOU

In 1984, I was a 20-year-old intern at Merck & Co., helping roll out the first IBM PCs. I carried machines from room to room and watched people who had never touched a computer figure out, slowly, that their work was about to change.

Most were skeptical. A few were excited. All of them had to decide whether to get ahead of the change or wait it out.

I've watched that same pattern repeat across 4 technology waves. The internet. The cloud. Cybersecurity. Now AI. Each one moved faster than the last. Each one required the same thing from business leaders: a decision about whether to get ahead of the change or manage the fallout from waiting.

After Merck, I spent 25 years building companies that helped businesses navigate those moments. In 2000 I started Entegration, an IT company focused on helping small and midsize businesses (SMBs) adopt the internet. I then founded HIPAA Secure Now to help medical practices get ahead of compliance before regulators arrived, and later started Breach Secure Now (BSN) to build security awareness training when ransomware started hitting small businesses with no defenses. Today, BSN trains more than 1 million employees across 35,000+ businesses in security awareness and AI readiness.

That experience across 4 technology waves shapes how I see this one. BSN is an SMB. We went through exactly what you're about to go through, and we had to build our own path because there was no guide for companies our size.

This book is the guide we didn't have.

The Problem You're Already In

Your people are already using AI. Not because you told them to, but because the tools are free, fast, and sitting in any browser. ChatGPT. Gemini. Perplexity. Most of your employees started at home and brought the habit to work on Monday morning.

You don't fully control what they're doing with it. Some of their usage may involve client data, financial records, or internal strategy going into public AI tools, outside your visibility, with limited control and no reliable way to reverse the exposure.

Your employees have already made the AI adoption decision. The leadership job now is to turn that unmanaged, invisible behavior into a safe, deliberate capability your organization can build on.

That's the job this book is designed to help you do.

What AI Actually Is

Before anything else, let me tell you what AI is. And I want to start with something you've already lived through.

Think about the last intern your company hired. You spent the first week getting them set up: accounts, introductions, a walkthrough of how things actually work (not how the manual says they work).

By week 3 they were drafting real deliverables, but everything needed a second pass. By month 3 they were genuinely useful, handling first drafts, pulling research, sitting in on calls and summarizing the takeaways.

By month 6 they knew your clients, your quirks, your standards. Then the internship ended. They walked out the door with everything you'd invested, and you started over with the next one.

Generative AI is that intern on the day they're finally good, except they don't graduate, they don't quit, and they don't take your institutional knowledge with them when they leave. It drafts emails, summarizes documents, researches competitors, writes first versions of almost anything, and helps you think through problems you'd normally stare at alone.

However, AI can't make the final call. It doesn't know your business the way you do. It needs direction, review, and a human who's responsible for what goes out the door.

That framing (AI as intern, not replacement) is the foundation everything in this book builds on.

What This Book Will Do

Tools change every 6 months. Anything written about a specific product will be dated by the time you read it. This is a book about the things that don't change: how people adopt new technology, how leaders create the conditions for that adoption to succeed, and how to build a culture where AI becomes a permanent part of how your business works.

By the end, you'll have a clear picture of where your organization stands, a 90-day plan to move it forward – including governance and safety precautions – and a framework for improvement that holds up as the technology keeps evolving.

The transformation is already happening in your business. This book is about making sure you're the one directing it.

1

HOW WE TRANSFORMED OUR COMPANY WITH AI

In November 2022, a colleague sent me a link to something called ChatGPT. The message said: "Try this. It's interesting."

Interesting was an understatement.

Within 10 minutes of typing my first prompt, I knew something had fundamentally changed. I've guided businesses through the internet, the cloud, and cybersecurity. None of those prepared me for what I was looking at. Here was a tool that could draft, analyze, and reason through problems at a level I'd never seen before. And it was sitting in a browser tab anyone could open for free.

Within weeks I had made a decision: BSN was going AI-first.

The Company We Were

At the time, BSN had about 90 employees. We were an online employee training platform serving more than 3,000 managed service providers (MSPs) and 20,000 small businesses, with over 750,000 employees using our security awareness and HIPAA training. By most measures, BSN was already a healthy, growing company.

We also had the friction that comes with growth. Content creation was slow and expensive. Sales research was manual and inconsistent. New hire onboarding took weeks before people became productive. Everyone was busy, but we weren't always sure we were busy on the right things.

None of those were crisis-level problems. They were the kind of steady drag that limits how fast a good company can move.

How We Rolled It Out

I started by buying ChatGPT Team licenses for our early adopters, the employees who were already curious and experimenting on their own. At the same time, I created an AI Acceptable Use Policy that let everyone use free tools with clear guidelines: what data was safe to put in, which tools were approved, and what human oversight looked like.

The policy was simple: experiment freely, but protect client data. Use AI to accelerate your work, and make sure a human is accountable for what goes out the door.

What happened next surprised me. Every week, more employees came asking for paid licenses. They'd started with the free tier, seen what was possible, and wanted the full version. Within 3 months we went from a handful of early adopters to visible company-wide momentum, and we got there without a single mandate.

We set up a Microsoft Teams channel for sharing prompts and discoveries. Friday collaboration meetings turned into show-and-tell sessions where people demonstrated what they'd figured out and celebrated each other's wins. The culture around AI shifted from something people were quietly doing on the side to something everyone was openly excited about.

The Immediate Results

Within the first 6 months, productivity gains showed up across every department. Content creation that used to take days now took hours. Contract review dropped from hours to minutes. Across our support operation, response times fell 62% while customer satisfaction increased 28%. Financial reporting that had required 2 full days now took only 4 hours, with deeper analysis than before.

Those speed improvements mattered. But the bigger shift was that AI started giving us capabilities we hadn't possessed before.

Capabilities We Didn't Have Before

For months, our MSP partners had been requesting Microsoft 365 training for their clients. Prior to this time, we didn't have the deep expertise or bandwidth to build it at scale. AI changed that. We used ChatGPT's Microsoft 365 knowledge to source curriculum and structure lessons, then layered in our own instructional design expertise. The result was a brand-new $1.2M+ annual revenue stream built faster than we could have assembled it manually.

Sales research went from 40 minutes per prospect to 5 minutes using Perplexity Pro. Our sales team walked into calls with real business intelligence: competitive analysis, company context, conversation starters. The sales cycle shortened 23%, and our close rate improved 31%.

We built our AI Awareness Training product using AI to accelerate the foundation work while our experts ensured quality. That became the standard model: AI moves fast, humans maintain credibility. It let us enter new markets and launch products faster than had ever been possible before.

The Part That Surprised Me Most

I expected productivity gains. The cultural shift caught me off guard.

Writers became better researchers. Analysts became clearer communicators. Support staff started solving problems proactively instead of reactively. People who had felt limited by the slow parts of their jobs suddenly felt capable of more. Employee satisfaction went up 34%. Retention improved 19%.

Across the first 2 years, revenue per employee rose 27%, operating margins improved 18%, and new hire productivity increased 45%. We did it with zero layoffs. We grew the business and grew the people at the same time.

What We Got Wrong Early

People don't all adopt at the same pace. Some employees dove in immediately. Others needed more time, more encouragement, and more support before they trusted the tools. Pressure didn't work. Meeting people where they already were was the secret.

We also didn't establish quality standards early enough. Early AI outputs were sometimes inconsistent or off-brand, which meant we had to build review processes and style guides retroactively. The lesson: set your quality bar before AI outputs start going out the door, not after.

And we didn't capture early wins systematically. Good stories got told verbally and disappeared. Once we started maintaining a shared library of effective prompts and successful use cases, adoption accelerated across teams that had been slower to experiment.

The 3 Things That Made It Work

Looking back, 3 factors drove the transformation.

First: I modeled the behavior personally. I used AI tools in meetings, shared prompts publicly, and made clear that experimentation wasn't just acceptable, it was expected. Culture change starts at the top. You can't ask your team to do something you aren't visibly doing yourself.

Second: we prioritized culture over technology. The tools were the easy part. Getting people to think differently about how they work took real effort. We built a safe environment for experimentation, created space to celebrate wins, and made learning collaborative rather than individual. That's what made adoption stick.

Third: we implemented ongoing training. We didn't just buy licenses and hope for the best. We ran continuous learning sessions, built prompt libraries, and set up peer mentoring. AI fluency requires practice. Organizations that treat training as a one-time event plateau fast, while those that continue the conversations level up exponentially.

What This Means for You

BSN is a business with real operations, real employees, and real challenges – the same ones you're navigating. The investment behind this transformation was modest: $20-50 per employee per month in tool licenses, 10 hours of training spread over 6 months, and roughly 5% of leadership time up front. Return on that investment showed up in weeks, not years.

Three Years In

Three years after going AI-first, here's where BSN stands.

We're using AI to automate as much as we can: implementing n8n, a workflow automation tool that connects our systems and triggers actions without manual intervention, building custom AI knowledge bases for sales and support, wiring it into the core of how the business runs. The tools are deeper now and the use cases are more ambitious.

The most meaningful shift is cultural. Our employees are raising their hands to ask for help automating parts of their own jobs. That's a different conversation than the one most businesses are having.

It took a full year of culture-building before we got there. From the start, I told employees directly that I wanted to embrace AI but had no intention of using it to reduce headcount. I said it early and often, until people believed it, and then we backed up that message with training for everyone.

We created awards for the most innovative use cases. We published dashboards showing pilots run, hours saved, and ROI achieved. Full transparency, updated regularly.

None of that is complicated, but it took effort, empathy, and time.

The result is a workforce that doesn't wait to be told where AI fits. They find it themselves and ask for help going further. That's what culture-first adoption produces.

PART 1

UNDERSTANDING

THE CHALLENGE

2

THE SHADOW AI REALITY

Shadow AI happens when well-meaning employees, trying to work faster and smarter, use personal AI tools for company work without your knowledge or approval. It often sits outside your normal security stack. And because it may run on personal smartphones and private browser windows, your IT team likely has little or no knowledge of its existence.

This chapter covers two distinct problems that AI has created simultaneously. The first is what your employees are doing with AI that creates risk. The second is what attackers can now do with AI against your employees. Both put your company at risk – one from the inside, one from the outside.

Part A: What Your Employees Are Doing

How It Started

It started at home.

Employees got comfortable with ChatGPT and Perplexity on personal tasks: looking up recipes, planning trips, searching for products, getting quick answers. The tools worked and they felt safe.

Then Monday morning arrived and the same habit came to the office.

The Scale of the Problem

75% of knowledge workers are already using AI on the job. Most are on personal accounts. Most haven't told their boss.[1,2]

ChatGPT alone now has nearly 1 billion weekly users as of early 2026.[3] The vast majority are using free consumer accounts, not the enterprise versions your company controls or can monitor.

For the last 10 years, businesses have been fighting to keep criminals out: firewalls, antivirus, threat detection. Layers of security have been built to stop someone from breaking in and taking what's yours.

Shadow AI added a new front. Criminals are still breaking in. But now your employees are also walking company data out the door, not maliciously, but habitually.

That's a different problem and it requires a different solution.

The Paste Problem

The most immediate risk is what happens when employees combine their AI habit with company data. An employee copies something from your systems, pastes it into a public chatbot,

---

[1] Microsoft and LinkedIn. "2024 Work Trend Index Annual Report: AI at Work Is Here. Now Comes the Hard Part." May 8, 2024. microsoft.com/en-us/worklab/work-trend-index/ai-at-work-is-here-now-comes-the-hard-part. The 75% figure applies to knowledge workers using AI at work; 78% bring their own tools (BYOAI).

[2] Fishbowl survey of 11,793 professionals, January–February 2023. Found 68% of those using AI at work had not informed their manager. Reported by Tech.co and multiple outlets, February 2023. The "without telling their boss" element in the manuscript draws on this survey, not the Microsoft/LinkedIn report.

[3] OpenAI announcement, February 27, 2026. ChatGPT reached 900 million weekly active users as of that date. The "nearly 1 billion" formulation reflects this figure plus Sam Altman's informal TED backstage disclosure (April 2025) that the platform had reached approximately 1 billion users. No formal press release confirmed the 1 billion milestone with a specific date stamp.

and asks AI to summarize, draft, or analyze. That data has now been transferred into a third-party AI environment your company doesn't control.

Here's what's getting pasted: client lists exported from CRMs for personalized outreach, sensitive pricing models for proposal drafting, internal financials for analysis, contracts and MSAs for plain-English summaries, customer support histories and personal data, and confidential employee reviews pasted in to "summarize the key points."

Every one of those is a transfer of company assets into someone else's infrastructure, with no reliable way to reverse the exposure.

The data leakage risk is the one most leaders think about. The bigger surprise is what's already running inside your business without anyone's approval.

MSPs auditing client environments for the first time consistently report the same shock: once you actually look, the number of unsanctioned AI tools running inside the business is far larger than anyone expected.

- AI note-takers scattered across departments, each recording and storing meeting data on servers you've never vetted.
- Chrome extensions installed by whoever clicked first in the search results, each with its own data trail and zero compliance posture.
- Productivity tools plugged directly into inboxes and calendars that IT never reviewed, never approved, and can't currently see.

One MSP put it plainly after completing a client audit: "We realized half the organization was using rogue AI tools we'd never even heard of."

That's a visibility failure. You can't govern what you can't see.

It's Already Happening

Samsung engineers accidentally exposed proprietary source code.[4] Amazon employees leaked internal operational data.[5] J.P. Morgan had client communications fed into public AI tools.[6]

Law firms and hospitals have seen the same thing.

These are documented cases. This has already happened at companies that thought they were protected.

The Consequences

Three categories of risk follow every unmanaged paste.

The first is data training. If it's free, you are the product. Consumer accounts on ChatGPT, Gemini, and similar platforms use your inputs to train their models and improve their outputs.

What that means in practice is that information your employees paste in today can surface in someone else's conversation later. Your trade secrets become training material. There's no retrieval option once that transfer happens.

There's a related risk most leaders don't consider. Not every AI tool that shows up in a Google search is a legitimate product.

---

[4] Samsung semiconductor division ChatGPT incidents, March 2023. Originally reported by *The Economist Korea*, March 30, 2023; confirmed and widely covered by *PC Magazine*, Mashable, and CS Hub, April 6, 2023.
[5] Amazon warning to employees regarding ChatGPT. *Business Insider*, January 23, 2023. An Amazon corporate lawyer warned staff not to share confidential information with ChatGPT after the company observed AI outputs that closely matched internal data.
[6] J.P. Morgan Chase restricted employee use of ChatGPT firm-wide. *Bloomberg* and *The Telegraph*, February 22, 2023. The restriction was described as preventive and part of normal third-party software controls; J.P. Morgan did not confirm a specific breach had occurred.

Some browser extensions, free summarizers, and "AI-powered" tools that employees install without IT review are built specifically to harvest the data entered into them.

That's a different problem from model training. It's deliberate data theft dressed up as a productivity tool.

The second is compliance. Entering PII or confidential client data into a public AI model can trigger immediate violations of HIPAA, GDPR, and the NDAs your clients signed with you.

Is your company's cyber insurance even valid for this kind of leak? Most policies were written before generative AI existed.

A recent federal court ruling made the compliance risk concrete. A judge ruled that 31 documents created using Claude AI aren't protected by attorney-client privilege.[7] The reasoning was direct: Claude isn't your lawyer, Anthropic owes you no duty of confidentiality, and their terms permit government access.

The moment you typed your legal strategy into that chat window, you disclosed it to a third party. In the court's view, privilege was lost.

From a confidentiality standpoint, the consumer-tier distinction may not protect you the way many users assume. Sam Altman, CEO of OpenAI, said it plainly: "There's no legal confidentiality when using ChatGPT."[8] The same applies to Claude and to Gemini.

Enterprise versions offer stronger protections, but most employees aren't using enterprise versions.

---

[7] United States v. Heppner, No. 25-cr-00503-JSR, U.S. District Court for the Southern District of New York. Oral ruling issued February 10, 2026 by Judge Jed S. Rakoff.
[8] Sam Altman, interview on "This Past Weekend with Theo Von," podcast, July 2025. Reported by *TechCrunch*, July 25, 2025.

The third is accuracy and liability. AI gets things wrong, *confidently*. If AI-generated content with false claims about a competitor ends up on your website or in a sales deck, the legal and reputational exposure is yours.

Part B: What Attackers Are Doing

The Attack Vector You Weren't Trained For

The security threat didn't stop at data leakage. AI changed how criminals attack your employees too.

For years, security training taught people to spot phishing through telltale signs: bad grammar, awkward phrasing, generic greetings. That playbook is obsolete.

82.6% of phishing emails now contain AI-generated content.[9] The tone matches the sender it's impersonating, the grammar is flawless, and the personalization is specific.

IBM researchers demonstrated that an AI can build a phishing campaign as effective as one crafted by human experts in 5 minutes using 5 prompts.[10] The same work used to take 16 hours.

What matters is not the exact number. It's that phishing quality and speed have both changed simultaneously.

---

[9] KnowBe4. "Phishing Threat Trends Report, 5th Edition." March 20, 2025. prnewswire.com. Found 82.6% of phishing emails analyzed exhibited some use of AI, based on data from September 2024 through February 2025.
[10] Stephanie Carruthers, "AI vs. Human Deceit: Unravelling the New Age of Phishing Tactics," IBM Security Intelligence blog, October 2023. IBM X-Force Red research.

AI-linked attacks have surged 1,265% since 2023.[11] Traditional phishing gets an already scary 12%[12] click-through rate, but AI-generated phishing ensnares 54% of us. That's more than half of all email users.

Your employees were never trained for this.

The deepfake threat is further along than most leaders realize.

In early 2024, a finance employee at Arup, the global engineering firm, transferred $25 million to fraudsters after attending what appeared to be a legitimate video conference with the company's CFO and senior leadership.[13] Every face was real. Every voice matched. *Every participant was AI-generated.*

62% of organizations faced a deepfake attack last year.[14] The average cost to create one is less than $2 and a voice can be cloned from as little as 3 seconds of audio.[15]

Any executive who has spoken at a conference or posted a video online has already provided the raw material for their own impersonation.

---

[11] SlashNext. "State of Phishing Report 2023." October 29, 2023. Found a 1,265% increase in malicious phishing emails over the 12 months from Q4 2022 to Q3 2023, attributed in part to the launch of ChatGPT.

[12] Fred Heiding, Bruce Schneier, et al. "AI-Automated Spear Phishing." arXiv:2501.05265, January 2025. Harvard Kennedy School / Avant Research Group. AI-automated phishing achieved a 54% click-through rate, matching human expert campaigns at approximately 1/30th the cost. Standard phishing achieved approximately 12% CTR.

[13] Arup finance worker deepfake incident, February 2024. Reported by multiple outlets including CNN, BBC, and *The Guardian.*

[14] Gartner survey of 302 cybersecurity leaders in North America, EMEA, and Asia-Pacific, March–May 2025. Published September 2025. Found 62% of organizations experienced a deepfake attack in the past 12 months.

[15] McAfee Labs. "AI Voice Scam Report." 2023. Found that 3 seconds of audio was sufficient to produce a voice clone with an 85% match. The "3 seconds" figure is the primary-source finding; "60 seconds" appears in secondary sources and is not the authoritative figure.

The same employee who pastes sensitive data into a public AI tool without thinking will trust an AI-generated phishing email for the same reason: they haven't been taught to stop and verify. The organization running unchecked Shadow AI is leaking data outbound while criminals use AI to craft targeted attacks inbound.

Culture is the new security perimeter.

Why Blocking Doesn't Work

The instinct is to ban AI in the workplace. That instinct is understandable but wrong.

If you block AI on your company network, employees will switch to their phones. 52% of workers say they'd still use AI even if their employer banned it – and among executives, that figure rises to 67%.[16] You risk going from limited visibility to zero visibility.

There's also a business cost. Every day your employees can't use AI at work, your competitors' employees can.

Blockbuster didn't lose because streaming was bad. It lost because it waited to adopt streaming. Banning AI is the same poor bet.

What actually works is giving people a path: approved tools, clear guardrails, and training that tells them exactly what they can do and why. That's what brings Shadow AI into the light.

Two Exposures, One Solution

AI has created 2 simultaneous exposures for every SMB: unmanaged data flowing out through employee habits, and

---

[16] CalypsoAI. "Insider AI Threat Report." August 12, 2025. Survey of over 1,000 U.S. office workers. Found 52% of employees would use AI even if it violated company policy; among executives specifically, this figure was 67%.

stronger, more convincing attacks coming in through AI-generated phishing and deepfakes.

They share a root cause. Employees who haven't been trained on what's safe don't know what to trust, in either direction. The same training that reduces Shadow AI also makes employees harder to fool.

The rest of this book is about building that training, those guardrails, and the culture that makes both stick.

3

WHY "DOING NOTHING" FAILS

Most leaders are waiting for clarity: a better tool, a clearer standard, a moment when the picture settles enough to make a confident call. That wait has a cost.

Doing nothing is not the absence of an AI strategy. It is the decision to let employees, default tool settings, and informal habits create one for you.

The "Ignore It" Trap

In the previous chapter, we established the baseline that 75% of knowledge workers are already using AI on the job, mostly on personal accounts, mostly without telling their boss.

The question was already answered before leadership got involved. The only question now is whether your organization will shape how it's being used in the future, or be forced into damage control for what happened while you were waiting.

When organizations honestly inventory their AI situation, the gaps are consistent: no written AI Acceptable Use Policy that employees have acknowledged, no formal training, no assessment of where data exposure is already happening, and often no visibility into which tools are being used at all.

That's the baseline for "doing nothing." The risk is already there.

When You Move Without a Plan

Waiting isn't the only way to fall behind. Moving without a plan gets you there just as fast.

A MetLife study put 2 numbers side by side that most AI rollouts ignore.[17] 83% of HR leaders say AI makes employees work faster. 67% say it's creating friction and mistrust in the workplace.

Both can be true at the same time.

Speed without training produces what researchers have started calling "workslop": AI-generated content that looks polished but lacks substance. It shifts cleanup work onto coworkers, strains collaboration, and erodes trust quietly enough that nobody flags it until the damage is already done.

For SMBs, the margin is thin. Small teams can't absorb a wave of low-quality AI output the way a large organization might.

When polished-looking work lands without substance, someone else carries the rework. On a 10-person team, that load becomes visible immediately.

ADP's chief economist framed it plainly: getting real value from AI requires business processes, change management, and upskilling.[18] The software license is the easy part.

---

[17] MetLife 24th Annual U.S. Employee Benefit Trends Study (EBTS). Published March 16, 2026. Survey of 2,480 HR decision-makers and 2,541 full-time employees, conducted October 2025 and January 2026.

[18] Nela Richardson, ADP Chief Economist. Remarks consistent with documented statements at the World Economic Forum 55th and 56th Annual Meetings (January 2025 and February 2026) and ADP Media Center publications. The specific formulation "the software license is the easy part" is a paraphrase of her documented thesis; exact wording requires verification against WEF transcript. WEF/ADP podcast: weforum.org/podcasts/meet-the-leader.

Rolling out tools without the training and culture plan to support them gets you behind just as fast, with the added cost of a workforce that's now skeptical of the next initiative you ask them to trust.

The Hidden Cost of Waiting

Every week without a policy is another week your employees are making their own calls about what's safe to paste into ChatGPT, what tools are okay to use, and what the company's actual position is. Most of them are guessing.

That gap turns everyday employee behavior into unmanaged company risk. Employees figuring this out on their own are making decisions you don't know about, with data you're responsible for. Every week in neutral is another week that risk compounds with no oversight.

The failure rate on AI pilots makes the cost of drifting clearer. MIT research found that 95% of corporate AI pilots fail to scale beyond initial testing.[19] Across AI projects broadly, 70 to 95% fail to deliver on their stated goals.

The common failure point isn't usually the software. It's the human system around it.

63% of organizations cite human factors as the primary challenge. When AI is rolled out *to* employees rather than *with* them, the response is resistance, regardless of how good the technology is.

Most pilots fail before the technology gets a fair test because the culture was never ready.

---

[19] MIT NANDA Initiative. "The GenAI Divide: State of AI in Business 2025." Published August 2025. Based on 150 executive interviews, survey of 350 employees, and analysis of 300 public AI deployments.

A pharmaceutical company's CIO purchased Microsoft Copilot licenses for 500 employees, paying roughly $180,000 in additional annual licensing costs.[20] After 6 months, he canceled the subscription. Employees hadn't received structured training to build real habits, and the legal team blocked one of the most useful features – meeting summaries – over liability concerns about retaining transcripts.

The tool wasn't the problem. The issue was that the rollout was treated like a purchase order rather than a tool for business advancement.

A *Wall Street Journal* profile featured Mike Salvatore, owner of Heritage Hospitality Group in Chicago (2 cafes, 2 bars, and a bike shop). He used to run cost-of-goods reports once or twice a year, spending hours crunching price adjustments manually. Now he does it every 3 weeks with ChatGPT.

The gap between "twice a year" and "every 3 weeks" is the cost of waiting, measured in pricing decisions your competitors are making while you're still running last quarter's numbers.

The Leadership Decision

Shadow AI is a leadership problem the moment something goes wrong and someone asks who was supposed to handle this.

Ultimately, someone has to define which tools are approved, what data can safely go into AI, and what employees are expected to do. For an SMB, that accountability lands with its leadership.

---

[20] Unnamed pharmaceutical company Copilot cancellation. Reported by *Business Insider*, July 2024; Morgan Stanley research note, 2024. CIO cited via Morgan Stanley analyst call transcript.

4

THE COST OF INACTION

The Employee Who Never Asked for This

Most employees are navigating AI without a map.

On one side: headlines about layoffs, job elimination, and hard-earned skills becoming obsolete. On the other: a relentless organizational push for AI tools, autonomous agents, and platforms designed to move faster with less human involvement.

Layer in the expectation that this is the biggest workplace shift in a generation. Then add the reality that most employees haven't received the training or context to operate in it.

Some colleagues are running. Others are still walking, waiting for someone to tell them what's expected. Every week without that clarity, the gap between them gets harder to close."

That's the environment your employees are sitting in when you announce your AI initiative. What they hear in that moment depends almost entirely on what you've done before it.

A workforce that's been prepared, given tools, guardrails, and a clear picture of how AI fits their role, hears opportunity.

A workforce that hasn't been prepared hears confirmation of every fear they already had.

Fear doesn't need much to take hold. Silence is enough.

Most employees aren't talking about the anxiety. But it's there, and it runs deeper than job replacement.

They're not just scared AI will make them redundant. They're scared of becoming completely unnecessary. Every podcast, conference, and LinkedIn feed says the same thing: adapt or get left behind.

The result is a workforce quietly spinning, trying to do the job they were hired for while feeling like they're already behind on tools they were never trained to use.

That fear is valid. Without leadership stepping in, the anxiety compounds quietly.

Encouraging people to use AI is a suggestion, not a strategy. Suggestions don't calm fear.

Structure does that. Your employees deserve clear guidance, real training, and a culture that shows them the organization is figuring this out together. That's what leadership owes its team.

Build the culture, give your people a path, so that fear stops driving the bus.

Three Ways Inaction Costs You

The cost of inaction compounds across 3 dimensions.

1. Security and Compliance

Chapter 2 covered this in detail. Every day without AI governance is a day your security and compliance exposure grows. The paste problem is already happening.

The only question is whether you're managing it or leaving it to chance.

2. Competitive Disadvantage

Chapter 3 covered the cost of waiting. The productivity gap is already opening. Businesses using AI are turning around proposals faster, cutting documentation overhead, and responding to customers in less time.

Every month of delay is a month of that advantage building on the other side of the table.

3. Cultural Erosion

This one is quieter and does more damage over time.

Inaction corrodes culture when employees know AI exists, use it privately, but can't use it openly at work. A hidden divide forms.

Some people are working smarter. Others are falling behind. If the organization stays silent, the gap keeps widening.

The usage gap between roles makes the cultural erosion concrete. AI adoption isn't evenly distributed across roles. Marketing and sales teams are already building daily habits with AI tools, while operations and administrative roles are barely using them. Same company, same tools, completely different levels of capability developing in parallel.

That's the two-speed company. Some employees are getting faster, sharper, and more capable every week. Others are left doing the same work the same old way.

The gap widens quietly if no one creates a forum to surface it.

Bain & Company documented this from inside their own firm.[21] They deployed ChatGPT Enterprise to 16,000 employees and Microsoft Copilot to roughly the same group. The result: 16,000 active ChatGPT users and about 2,000 active Copilot users, inside the same organization, with the same people, using the same devices.

---

[21] Bain & Company internal AI deployment. Reported by *Bloomberg*, June 2025. Supporting detail in Bain & Company published case study, "Bain & Company's Journey: Speeding Up AI Adoption," October 2024.

Their CTO attributed the difference to adoption design, not technology quality.

The ChatGPT rollout came with a sponsorship structure, office champions, and real use cases tied to daily work. Copilot came with access only. Access without culture produces exactly this: a visible divide between the tool that got *support* and the tool that got *installed*.

The people most likely to leave are the ones in the fast lane, aware enough to know when a company is falling behind. Unfortunately, the people most likely to stay are the ones least equipped to help you grow.

The competitive cost isn't always abstract. Amazon adjusts prices millions of times a day using AI. Online retailers who adopt dynamic pricing tools are capturing sales from competitors still running static price sheets updated quarterly.

That's already the reason some businesses are losing deals they never even knew were in play.

The cost of inaction is clear. Now it's time for Part 2, where you build the culture that turns AI from a risk into a working advantage.

PART 2
BUILDING
YOUR AI-READY
CULTURE

5

THE THREE PILLARS OF AI CULTURE

Most AI rollouts follow the same sequence. Leadership picks a tool, announces it, runs one training session, and waits for employee adoption to happen.

The tool isn't the problem. Access isn't either. What's missing is the positive culture around the tool, including whether people feel safe experimenting, whether wins get shared or hoarded, and whether AI gets treated as a genuine work tool or a side project IT manages.

An AI-ready culture rests on 3 interconnected dimensions: Mindsets, Behaviors, and Systems. Build one without the other 2 and it doesn't hold. Build all 3 and AI adoption stops being a project someone has to manage; it becomes how work gets done.

Pillar 1: Mindsets

This is how your employees think about AI. Their mindset varies depending on where they sit in the organization, and each level needs a different frame.

Leaders see AI as a strategic tool for business growth. Every conversation about AI at the leadership level should connect back to an outcome: efficiency, capacity, competitive position, client experience. Leaders who treat it as a tech curiosity instead of a business tool leave most of its value on the table.

Managers see AI as a way to make their teams more capable and productive. When a manager sees a repetitive task eating 2 hours a week, the instinct should be: "Can AI handle part of this?" Their job is identifying those opportunities and creating conditions where people can work smarter.

Employees can see AI as a threat. A more helpful framework is for employees to view AI as a digital intern. Human interns take first passes at drafts, do research, summarize meetings, and pull together information so experienced people can focus on judgment, relationships, and decisions. AI can efficiently handle these same necessary and time-consumptive tasks.

It is critical to remember, however, that all interns get things wrong sometimes, and it is necessary for a human to catch the error. When employees understand that frame, the fear of replacement starts to fade.

Each level reinforces the others: leaders set the direction, managers build the habits, and employees do the work.

When all 3 see AI through the right lens, workplace culture starts to move.

The division of labor looks like this:

AI Intern Does	Employee Does
Generate first drafts	Direct and provide context
Summarize long documents	Review and validate accuracy
Suggest options and ideas	Make final decisions
Reformat and structure data	Ensure quality and completeness

The 2 Traps to Avoid

When employees don't have a clear frame for what AI is, they fall into 1 of 2 traps. Both cost you.

The first is over-trust. The employee pastes in a question, accepts the output without reading it carefully, and sends it out. This is how hallucinated statistics end up in proposals and fabricated details end up on your website.

The intern gave you something that sounded confident. Nobody checked.

The second is under-use. The employee is afraid of looking lazy, doing it wrong, or getting caught depending on a tool they don't fully understand. So they skip it entirely and grind through the same work manually, even when the tool could cut the time in half.

The intern mindset solves both. It sets the expectation that AI is capable but needs supervision. That combination is what makes confident, safe adoption possible.

Not every employee cares about AI deeply, and that's fine. Some people will use ChatGPT occasionally to draft an email or look something up and never go further. There are a lot of people like that in every SMB.

The intern mindset works for them precisely because it doesn't ask them to care about AI. It asks them to think of it as a tool that handles the tedious parts of a job. Keep the adoption plan calibrated to where most people are, not to the early adopters.

The Microsoft 365 Parallel

The intern analogy handles the question employees are really asking themselves: is AI going to take my job?

Microsoft Word gave writers a faster way to write. Excel gave accountants sharper analysis. PowerPoint gave presenters a way to make their ideas visible.

None of those tools did the work on their own.

The tool simply amplified the person. The person gave the tool its value.

AI works exactly the same way. The message still comes from you. The interpretation is still yours.

AI can help develop an idea, but it requires human judgment to decide what matters.

When someone on your team asks whether AI is going to replace them, address the fear directly. Learning to use AI makes employees both more capable and more valuable. Skipping it means falling behind other employees who can do the same work faster.

That message is more convincing when it comes directly from a manager rather than from a memo.

Pillar 2: Behaviors

Mindsets only matter if they show up in how people actually work. The behaviors you're looking for are specific and observable.

Employees will ideally reach for the AI tool at the start of a task, not after they've already done it the hard way. Afterward, they can share prompts that worked in the same way they'd share any useful shortcut.

Managers can ask, "Did you try AI on this?" the way they'd ask any reasonable process question. Through repetition, the question reminds employees that AI tools exist and are welcome in your company, within the parameters set out by your acceptable use policy.

Make sure the wins get mentioned publicly: how someone cut a 3-hour report to 45 minutes, or drafted 5 client follow-ups in the same time it used to take to write 1. Visible usage is what a healthy AI culture actually looks like. When people are open about what works and what doesn't, the whole organization learns faster.

Shadow AI is a behavior problem too. When people hide their usage, it's almost always because they're unsure if they're allowed, or worried what their manager will think. Those behaviors only change when the mindset and the systems are already in place.

Pillar 3: Systems

Even the right mindsets and behaviors break down without systems that support them. Systems turn individual adoption into organizational capability.

These 3 systems matter most.

The first is *tools*. Provide approved AI applications your employees know they can use for work. When people understand exactly which AI tools are safe for company data, they stop improvising with personal free accounts. One clear list removes a lot of friction.

The second is *training*, and this is where most organizations underinvest. Baseline AI awareness for every employee is the starting point, but one-time training doesn't hold. Chapter 7 will cover the full training architecture, including why it has to be continuous, why it has to be role-specific, and how to build the structure that makes both possible.

The third is *guardrails*. Create plain-language rules about what data is appropriate for AI, which tasks fit well, and what to do when something goes wrong. Guardrails exist to make the right behavior the default behavior.

When all 3 of these systems are in place, the path of least resistance becomes the right path.

The 4 Shifts That Move a Culture

The 3 pillars above describe what an AI-ready culture looks like when it's working. The shifts below describe how you get there. They don't happen on a schedule and they don't all happen at once.

Knowing what to watch for helps you see whether the culture is actually moving.

1. From Fear to Experimentation

Most employees approach new technology with the same question: *Is this going to make me look bad?* AI adds a second layer of fear and anxiety: *Is this going to make me unnecessary?*

Those concerns don't disappear because of a policy announcement. They dissolve through repeated small experiences where experimentation is safe, mistakes are treated as data, and trying something that doesn't work doesn't become a career-ending event.

The signal employees are watching for isn't in what leadership says about AI. It's in how leadership responds when someone tries something and it fails.

Create explicit permission to experiment. Celebrate *attempts*, not just *successes*. When a pilot produces a bad output, the question should be "what did we learn," not "who approved this?" That pattern of constructive behavior, repeated enough times, shifts the baseline from avoidance to curiosity.

2. From Secret to Shared

By the time most organizations launch a formal AI program, a significant portion of the workforce is already experimenting on their own. Prompts that work, workflows that save time, use cases nobody thought to try: all of it stays locked in individual experience rather than becoming organizational knowledge.

The positive shift happens when AI usage becomes a normal thing for your employees to talk about. This could look like a Teams channel where people share what worked and what didn't, quick demos in staff meetings, or a manager who asks people to show the workflow, not just the result.

When sharing becomes the default, learning compounds across the organization instead of staying siloed.

3. From Perfect to Progressive

Early AI outputs are often disappointing: the draft is generic, the summary misses the point. A lot of organizations hit that moment and conclude the tool doesn't work.

This expectation is skewed, however. Remember that AI produces a capable first draft, not a finished product. The value is in how much faster you and your team can get to a starting point, bypassing the painful blank screen.

When quality control is built around human review rather than AI perfection, the productivity gains show up and the frustration (mostly) disappears.

4. From Individual to Organizational

Individual employees discovering AI use cases on their own is a wonderful starting place, but it's not a helpful destination for the long-term. When adoption stays at the individual level, it's fragile. One person leaves and their prompts, their workflows, and their accumulated knowledge go with them.

The shift is moving AI fluency from personal skill to organizational capability: prompt libraries anyone can access, AI workflows documented as SOPs, onboarding that includes AI training from day one.

When we made this shift at BSN, adoption accelerated across teams that had been slower to implement. The employees who'd figured things out stopped being isolated experts. They became the foundation everyone else built on.

That's when AI ceases being a skill only a few people have and becomes part of how the entire company works.

6

LEADERSHIP'S CRITICAL ROLE

Your people are watching what you do with AI more than they're listening to what you say about it. If you send a policy memo but never visibly touch the tools yourself, the message lands as: this is something IT handles. If you praise the concept in a town hall but never narrate your own use, the message lands as: this is optional.

Culture moves from the top, which means AI adoption either gets modeled by leadership or it stalls.

There are 3 jobs leaders have in an AI rollout. None of them require being a technical expert.

Why This Starts With You, Not IT

Most AI rollouts start with an IT conversation. That's the wrong starting point.

Handing AI to IT is a leadership mistake that compounds quietly. While IT can deploy tools, manage access, and handle security, identifying where your sales team wastes 3 hours a day, where customer service breaks down, or where bad information drives bad decisions is a different job.

That's a leadership call.

When AI sits inside IT, the rest of the company assumes it's not their problem. The conversation shifts from growth to control. The tool gets installed, but employee behavior never changes.

Real adoption shows up in results: time saved, faster decisions, less friction. That starts with leaders identifying the right targets, not having IT pick the right platform.

The best AI use cases come from frontline employees who know exactly where the work is broken. Go find those people first. When you do, here's what you'll hear:

Your office manager spends 6 hours a week reformatting the same reports for different audiences. The AI intern does it in minutes.

Your sales team spends 40 minutes researching each prospect before a call. AI cuts that to 5.

HR sorts through 200 resumes to find 10 worth reading. AI builds the shortlist in an afternoon.

Your ops lead has 15 undocumented processes locked in their head. AI turns a rough brain dump into a clean SOP in 20 minutes.

Those aren't hypothetical. They're the kinds of wins that show up in the first 30 days when leaders ask the right people the right questions.

IT should enable AI, but leadership should own it.

The Corporate Governance Institute ran multiple small AI pilots before any of them scaled.[22] Their head of AI and technology described the pattern plainly: AI initiatives were being done in silos primarily driven by the tech team, and many were unsuccessful due to lack of adoption.

---

[22] Boris Geršić, Head of AI & Technology, The Corporate Governance Institute. Published case study: "AI Strategy for Business Leaders: From Siloed Projects to AI-Ready Culture." Code Institute, 2026.

The fix wasn't a new tool. It was developing a business-wide strategy with cross-functional ownership, identifying what AI was supposed to do for the business, not just how to deploy it.

Once leadership owned the direction, the same technical team that had been running unsuccessful pilots started running successful ones.

Job 1: Use AI Yourself, Visibly

The fastest way to signal that AI is real work, not a side experiment, is to use it where people can see you.

Here's what that looks like in practice. Most mornings I'm generating ideas faster than I can do anything with them. The workflow is simple: voice-type into my phone's notes app, then send that raw text into ChatGPT, which turns it into a first draft of whatever I need.

The whole thing takes a fraction of the time it used to.

When I have an idea for a landing page or a new product feature, I build a working prototype directly instead of handing marketing a description and hoping the idea survives the handoff. My team can see it, interact with it, and build from there.

I also use an AI avatar called Artemis to convert text posts into short videos for LinkedIn. The practical return is my time. But the more interesting outcome has been internal: when employees see me using AI openly and explaining how it works, AI starts to feel like something people here do.

Before a meeting with a long pre-read, I paste the document in and ask for a briefing:

> *"Here's a 12-page pre-read for tomorrow's strategy meeting. Give me a plain-language summary in 5 bullet points: what's being proposed, what it costs,*

what the risks are, and what decision is being asked for.”

That takes 30 seconds and gets me a summary I can scan before the meeting starts. When I walk in and say, “I had the intern summarize this,” I've just shown my team what using AI at work looks like.

The Leadership Blind Spot

There's a failure mode that comes with moving fast on AI personally, and I've lived it.

I jump between ChatGPT, Perplexity, Claude, Gemini, and NotebookLM throughout the day. It's made me faster than I've ever been. I take rough ideas and use these tools to flesh them out, go deeper, move faster.

Then I dump all of it on my employees.

Nobody told me it was *too much*. But I noticed. Slowly, my team stopped responding to every new idea.

The firehose was the problem, not the ideas.

As employees become more proficient with AI, this dynamic shows up everywhere. Ideas come faster. Content multiplies.

The individual velocity goes up but the organizational capacity to absorb it doesn't keep pace.

The lesson here is simple: using AI personally without building conditions the organization can absorb creates overhead, not acceleration. Build a culture in your company that channels overall AI productivity, not just one that celebrates your own efficiency.

Job 2: Narrate What You're Doing and Why

Silent AI use creates a vacuum. Your team will fill that void with their own assumptions, usually negative ones.

There's also a bigger problem leaders underestimate: signal loss. A CEO's vision is clear in their own head. As it moves through layers of management, nuance fades.

Teams interpret differently. Departments execute differently. The original idea arrives diluted.

What AI changed for me is my ability to send the original. Not a description of what I meant, but the actual thing: a whitepaper that lays out the argument the way I see it, or a short video walking through the thinking step by step.

These get much closer to the original idea than a secondhand summary ever could. The conversation changes completely when the starting point is something concrete rather than something described.

Narrating the process matters as much as doing it. When you share an AI-assisted document and explain how you made it, you do 2 things at once: you reduce signal loss on that specific idea, and you show your team that the tools work for this kind of thinking.

Say out loud what you're doing: "I used AI to draft this, then edited it" or "Treat AI like an intern on this one: have it draft and summarize, then you review before it goes anywhere."

Said once in the right moment, those lines give your team permission to experiment without feeling like they're doing something unofficial.

Job 3: Shape What Gets Praised and Corrected

People watch what gets recognized and what gets quietly let slide. Your job is to make the pattern clear.

When your ops lead says, "We started using the AI tool to draft SOPs and it cut our time in half," that's the moment. Respond publicly: "That's exactly how the digital intern is supposed to work. Can you share your process with the team?" You've just told everyone in the room what good looks like.

On the flipside, when you find out someone pasted internal financials into a personal AI account, correct it without making it a career event: "I get why you did it, but that's exactly the kind of data we keep out of personal tools. Next time, use the approved tool and ask before you paste if you're not sure."

A non-punitive correction teaches the behavior and the alternative at the same time, without undoing all the positive progress your company has made.

Over time, this pattern shapes your business' AI culture more than any policy document ever could.

The Job Security Conversation

Every person on your team is thinking it. *Is this going to take my job?* Most leaders skip the conversation because it's uncomfortable.

Skipping it tells your team exactly where leadership stands.

Address it directly. Here's what honest sounds like:

> "Our goal is to use AI to create leverage for every person here. That means it's also on you to upskill and make yourself more valuable. We're committed to giving you the tools and training to do that.

The question worth asking isn't "Am I safe?" It's "How do I get better?"

It also helps to know what the data shows, because your employees almost certainly don't. A recent Oxford Economics briefing found that companies aren't replacing workers with AI on a significant scale.[23] Even layoffs described as AI-related remain a small fraction of overall job losses.

Employees don't hear that nuance, however. They hear "Amazon laid off 14,000 people." The gap between what the research shows and what people believe is where the fear lives.

I can tell you what persistence and consistency look like in this approach. When I made the commitment to go AI-first, I told my employees directly: "AI is not here to replace you." I repeated this message until people believed it.

Three years later, no BSN employee has been laid off because of AI. What changed is our hiring pace: as employees became more capable with AI, the need to add headcount slowed. The people already on our team became even more valuable.

Your own track record will become the most convincing argument you can make.

When Some People Still Won't Come Around

No matter how well you create an AI-positive culture in your company, some people still won't come around. Most leadership advice on this topic skips that, so it's worth saying plainly.

Some employees will stay skeptical no matter what you do, and that's okay. What you need is critical mass, not unanimous buy-in. Once enough people are using AI openly and well, it will

---

[23] Oxford Economics, "Evidence of an AI-Driven Shakeup of Job Markets Is Patchy." Research briefing, January 7, 2026.

start to feel like normal work rather than a test some employees are failing.

That means 2 things in practice. You must take the concerns seriously. First, listen and address what you reasonably can, and don't be dismissive about worries that are genuinely worth having. Second, don't let resistance set the pace for everyone else. An employee who won't engage with approved tools can't quietly become the reason their team doesn't either.

As pilots run and wins get shared, most reluctance shifts on its own. People who were skeptical in week 2 are often asking for expanded access by week 10. The ones who stay resistant after all of that are a management question, not an AI question.

Your 30-Day Leadership Commitment

This chapter is most useful if it ends with a decision, not a concept.

Use AI in your own work at least once a week, visibly, and mention what you used it for. Talk about it in at least 2 team settings and reinforce the digital intern framework each time. Recognize at least 2 smart AI uses by your team by name, and ask them to share their process.

That's the full commitment. Start there.

7

HR AS THE CULTURE ENGINE

Chapter 5 established why culture matters more than tools. This chapter is about the mechanism that builds it inside your organization.

Not every SMB has a dedicated HR person, so if yours doesn't, this chapter belongs to whoever owns people and culture in your organization: an office manager, a COO, an operations lead, or the owner doing it all.

The job function matters more than the title.

Anyone can buy the same AI tools you're buying. ChatGPT, Copilot, Gemini are all a credit card away. What competitors can't replicate is a workforce that's confident, capable, and genuinely excited to use AI tools.

Training is also one of the most effective entry points for AI adoption. Done right, it doesn't feel like a mandate. It feels like investment: leadership taking the job security question seriously and actually doing something about it.

Employees who understand AI's capabilities and limits, who know which tools are safe and how to prompt them effectively, don't need to be pushed into adoption, because they're already using it, correctly, and with confidence.

The 3 Layers of Effective AI Training

Effective AI training has 3 layers that build on each other.

The first is fundamental training. This is where most organizations underinvest and where the foundation either holds or breaks. Fundamental training covers 2 things together:

1. How to think about AI
2. How to work with it

The mindset piece is the digital intern framework: AI as a capable assistant you direct, review, and stay accountable for. When employees internalize that approach, the fear of replacement starts to fade and the habit of reaching for AI starts to form.

The practical piece is prompting: how to give AI context, how to refine outputs, and how to offload the right tasks. It also covers guardrails like what data is safe to put in, which tools are approved, and what to do when something goes wrong.

A policy employees click through once doesn't change behavior. Training on the guardrails does. Most organizations get the policy right but skip the practice.

The second is role-specific application: the sales team uses AI for prospect research and outreach drafts, marketing creates campaign content with it, HR drafts job descriptions and employee communications, and finance uses it to build trend summaries and report drafts. This layer creates momentum. Once employees see their peers in other departments getting real results, adoption spreads on its own.

The third layer of effective training is ongoing learning. Because AI tools change fast, a one-time module might handle the baseline but will leave everything else to chance.

The half-life of AI skills is shrinking. Current estimates put it at roughly two years, down dramatically from a decade ago.[24,25] HR's job is to make learning continuous and role-specific so the organization doesn't plateau the moment the first training cycle ends.

The gap between what employees need and what most organizations provide is wider than many leaders realize.

A McKinsey survey of 3,600 employees puts a number on something HR leaders already sense.[26]

- 48% say formal training is the single most important thing that would change how they use AI at work. Nearly half say they've received almost none.

- 51% cite cybersecurity as their top AI concern: deepfakes, AI-generated phishing, scams that are getting harder to detect. 50% worry about inaccuracy.

They already sense the risk. They just don't have anyone helping them navigate it. The training gap is yours to close.

Leadership sets the direction on AI. HR builds the infrastructure that makes it real. The most critical piece of that infrastructure is training, so tell your people what to do, how to do it, and that it's safe to try.

---

[24] *World Economic Forum.* "Future of Jobs Report 2025." Published January 2025.

[25] Gartner/Workera estimate on AI skills half-life. Kian Katanforoosh (Stanford/Workera), reported in *Forbes*, April 2024: AI-specific skills half-life "as short as two years," down from approximately 10 years for general skills. Gartner LinkedIn post, March 2026: "By 2030, the half-life of technical skills will shrink to just two years." The "3-4 months" figure that circulates in AI upskilling content lacks a confirmed primary source.

[26] McKinsey & Company. "Superagency in the Workplace: Empowering People to Unlock AI's Full Potential at Work." January 2025. Survey of 3,613 employees and 238 C-level executives, October–November 2024.

What HR Should Avoid

Before getting to the levers that make AI adoption stick, here is a short list of what *not* to do.

- Don't treat AI training as a one-off compliance module. Skills keep changing and a single session can't keep up. The training has to be continuous or it ceases to be useful.

- Don't make the messaging so polished it feels like "spin." Employees can tell when the communication is designed to manage their reaction rather than inform it. Clear beats clever.

- Don't let managers improvise different answers on job security and acceptable use. If employees are getting 4 different stories depending on who their manager is, the policy is functionally meaningless. Align the message before it goes out the door.

5 Levers That Determine Whether Adoption Sticks

Lever 1: Communication

Most employees are filling in the blanks about AI on their own right now. They're reading headlines, talking to each other, and drawing their own conclusions about what their company's AI push means for their job. HR's first task should be to replace that silence with a clear, consistent story.

That story has several parts.

The first is the why: AI helps people work smarter, take repetitive tasks off their plates, and spend more time on the work that requires human judgment, creativity, and relationships.

The second is the role: the digital intern framework, and what it means for how people work with AI day to day.

The third is the commitment: the organization is putting real tools and real training behind the words.

The fourth is the expectation: learn the basics, use AI where it makes sense, and always review what the AI intern produces before it goes anywhere.

That message, delivered clearly and repeated consistently, is what actually reduces Shadow AI.

Lever 2: Onboarding

If AI is going to feel normal instead of optional, it needs to show up before the first week. Job postings that mention AI fluency signal culture to candidates before they apply. Interview questions like "How have you used AI in your work?" tell candidates what the organization values before they accept an offer.

The people who self-select in will already be oriented the right way.

New employees set their baseline for "how we work here" in the first 30 days. Miss that window and AI becomes something people discover on their own later, often through Shadow AI.

A standard AI onboarding package starts with a short message from leadership explaining the company's AI philosophy, paired with baseline AI and security awareness training. Round it out with a one-pager covering approved tools and guardrails, and a manager follow-up in the first week to reinforce the message in plain language.

The same tools that train new hires also help you find them. HR teams spend hours writing and rewriting job descriptions from scratch. Instead, hand it to the intern:

"Draft a job description for a [role title] at a [industry] company with [X] employees. Include 5 core responsibilities, 3 required qualifications, and 2 preferred qualifications. Keep it under 300 words, skip the corporate jargon."

That gets you a clean first draft in under a minute. Edit it into your voice, add the details only you know, and post it. When your new hire arrives and sees the team already using AI this way, the message is clear before anyone says a word.

The goal on day one is awareness. Make sure new employees know what's approved, what's expected, and where to go with questions.

Lever 3: Ongoing Learning

A one-time training module handles the baseline but leaves a gap everywhere else. By the time employees complete an AI course, the tools it covers may already be outdated.

HR's job is to make learning continuous and role-specific.

The structure that works has multiple tiers. The first is a baseline for everyone of annual AI awareness and security refreshers that keep the fundamentals current. Next is role-based micro-learning: short, targeted lessons built around what each department actually does. Not generic AI content, but task-level guidance for the work people are already doing.

Another tier is just-in-time resources: quick guides and short videos people can pull up when they hit a specific task. Generic AI literacy content is easy to produce and easy to ignore. Role-specific, task-level guidance is what people actually finish and use.

Managers play a role here too. The following questions, when asked consistently, will do more for ongoing learning than most formal programs: "Where did AI save you time this week?" and "Where did AI get something wrong that we learned from?"

One cost doesn't show up in productivity dashboards. New research found that 14% of AI users are experiencing what researchers call "AI brain fry" – mental fog from constant task-switching, continuous oversight, and the cognitive weight of managing AI outputs on top of doing an actual job.[27] High performers are getting hit hardest.

The oversight burden is the main driver. Supervising multiple AI outputs produces a 12% spike in mental fatigue and 33% greater information overload. Exhausted employees are 10% more likely to quit.

For SMBs this lands in a specific way. Employees are managing AI tools they were never trained to manage. That cognitive overhead lands on people who were already stretched. Unprepared workforces absorb the overhead of AI adoption and carry it as cognitive load, not productivity.

Train the people, or the tools will bury them.

Lever 4: Guardrails

HR partners with IT and leadership to answer the following questions for employees in plain language:

- What tools are approved for work?
- What data can safely go into AI?
- What do you do when something goes wrong or you're genuinely unsure?

---

[27] Julie Bedard, Matthew Kropp, et al. "When Using AI Leads to 'Brain Fry'," *Harvard Business Review*, March 2026. Research conducted by Boston Consulting Group. Survey of 1,488 full-time U.S. workers.

These questions sound simple, however their answers are almost never written down anywhere employees can actually find them.

That gap is where Shadow AI insinuates itself. When people have to guess whether it's okay to paste a client email into ChatGPT, some guess yes and some guess no, and worst of all… neither group asks first.

The mistake-handling piece matters as much as the rules themselves. Employees need to know they can report a mistake immediately, without fear of punishment. When people are afraid to admit they shared something they shouldn't have, they hide it. And Shadow AI stays in the dark.

Chapter 10 will offer an easily implemented tool – the Traffic Light System – for data classification in detail. HR's role is to take that framework and translate it into language normal humans can understand, then put it somewhere people will actually look, and make sure every manager can explain it in a 2-minute conversation.

Lever 5: Psychological Safety

The previous 4 levers build the structure. This one determines whether people actually use it.

Psychological safety around AI means employees allow themselves to admit they don't understand something, ask for help, speak up when AI gets something wrong, and report issues without embarrassment or penalty.

HR can't manufacture moments like that. But it can create the environment where they become both normal and safe. That starts with how managers talk about AI day-to-day.

One of the more unexpected lessons from our own rollout came from my AI avatar, Artemis. When I started using the AI avatar publicly, including on team calls and in company communications, at first I was solving a time problem. What happened instead was that making AI visible and slightly absurd did more to lower employee resistance than any memo we'd written.

Employees who had been quietly skeptical started asking how it worked. A few built their own avatars. The conversation shifted from "Is AI going to replace us?" to "What can I make with this?"

That shift came from watching leadership use the tools openly, imperfectly, and without pretending to have it all figured out. HR creates the conditions for that to happen more often.

HR can reinforce this through engagement surveys that include AI-specific questions like "I understand how I'm expected to use AI in my job" and "I feel safe asking questions about AI tools." The answers will surface where the culture is strong and where it's fragile before those gaps turn into Shadow AI problems.

Frame AI as a skill the organization is building together, and people will be far more likely to lean in. HR is the organizational function best equipped to make that shift real.

Where HR Fits in the 90-Day Plan

The levers above are HR's contribution to Phase 1. The full 90-day sequence, with templates and timelines, is in Part 5 of this book. That's where your plan becomes operational.

If a new hire joins next week, will they learn about AI at your company by design or by accident?

HR is the difference.

8

Operations and Real Workflows

This chapter is about turning AI from a cultural concept into a workflow decision.

Culture meets reality in operations, where customers get served, tickets get closed, and work either flows or clogs. The chapters before this one built the mindset and the infrastructure. This one is about putting the digital intern to work.

The Visibility Problem

Before you can improve work with AI, you have to see it.

As a CEO, I'll be direct about something most leaders won't say out loud: I don't have clear visibility into what my employees do at the task level every day. I know they work hard and I know they produce quality output.

What's largely invisible to me is the daily workflow, the specific sequence of steps each person takes to get there.

Managers are closer to their teams, but if you ask a manager to map, document, and prioritize the workflows of every person they oversee, you will have created a project that stalls before it starts.

Employees know their own workflows best. But many won't document them willingly. There's real fear in mapping exactly what you do every minute of the day. It can feel like handing someone the blueprint to replace you. That's the same fear this book has been addressing throughout, and it shows up here in a very practical form.

Process visibility is what stands between AI potential and AI results. Most organizations can't see what work actually looks like at the task level, which means they're making automation decisions based on assumptions rather than reality.

The trust work recommended here – the culture, the training, the honest leadership conversations – is the prerequisite to gaining buy-in from your team. Employees won't map their workflows accurately in an environment where they're afraid of what the map will be used for.

The AI-positive culture has to come first. Then the visibility becomes possible.

Start With What's Already There

While you're building that foundation, there's a move available right now that requires no new processes, no policy decisions, and no significant training.

Every major AI platform now has some form of deep research capability built in: ChatGPT, Claude, Gemini, Perplexity, Copilot. The tools are often free or close to it, but most teams aren't using it deliberately.

This won't replace workflow redesign, but it gives teams an immediate way to get value while the larger work takes shape.

- Sales reps can walk into prospect meetings knowing a company's recent earnings, leadership changes, and competitive pressures.

- Marketing can track competitor positioning in real time.

- Operations can research vendor alternatives before contract renewals instead of after.

- Customer success can understand a client's industry challenges before a QBR instead of winging it.

None of that requires a redesigned workflow. It requires knowing how to ask.

The bigger shift is access. Information that used to live behind expensive research subscriptions or years of accumulated experience is now available to everyone on the team. Your junior account manager can prep like your VP of Sales.

Start here. The tools are already on their desks.

How to Pick Good AI Pilot Processes

Good pilot candidates are digital and text-heavy: emails, documents, tickets, or forms. They're also repetitive and frequent, usually daily or weekly, and they follow a clear structure or pattern.

Two other signals make a process worth piloting:

- You can quickly tell if AI got it right

- People already complain about it

That last one matters. If the task is annoying but necessary, adoption almost takes care of itself.

(Appendix E has a Pilot Selection Checklist with a "Sweet Spot" test and a "Red Flag" test to walk any process candidate through before you commit.)

The 5-Step AI Pilot Framework

Step 1 — Define the Process and Owner

What process are we targeting? Who owns it? What does success look like?

(e.g., "Cut time per task in half" or "Reduce back-and-forth emails by 30%")

Step 2 — Design the AI-Assisted Workflow

Map the current process in 4-6 steps. Mark which steps AI will help with (usually drafting, summarizing, or reformatting). Create 1 or 2 standard prompts everyone will use.

Step 3 — Enable the Pilot Team

Choose 3-10 people who actually do the work. Give them access to approved tools, a short training, and clear data guardrails.

Step 4 — Run the Pilot (30-60 Days)

Track how long the process takes compared to before, then save examples of good AI output, and flag cases where AI failed or needed heavy editing.

Step 5 — Review, Decide, and Document

Gather before vs. after metrics, examples, and suggestions. Decide: Scale (make it standard), Tweak (adjust and try again), or Drop (document why and move on).

3 Pilot Examples You Can Steal

Sales: Post-Call Follow-Up Emails

One of our sales reps was spending 20-30 minutes after every discovery call writing follow-up emails. She'd review her notes, decide what to highlight, then draft something from scratch. Quality varied depending on how tired she was and how many calls she'd already done that day.

We gave her a standard prompt to take the call notes, paste them in, and ask the AI to draft a follow-up email.

"Here are my notes from a discovery call with [company]. Draft a follow-up email under 150 words. Highlight the top 3 takeaways from the call, reference one specific pain point they mentioned, and propose a clear next step. Professional but conversational tone."

She edits and sends.

The draft takes about 2 minutes. She spends another 3-5 editing it into her voice. Her follow-up volume went up, response rates held steady, and she stopped dreading the post-call administrative work that used to bleed into her evenings.

That's the pattern: AI handles the first draft, then the human makes it real.

Support: Ticket Summaries for Escalations

Support agents at most SMBs spend 10-15 minutes writing escalation summaries for every complex ticket. The summaries vary by writer, and engineers frequently bounce them back with questions because the context is incomplete.

The AI-assisted fix is simple. Give the agent a prompt that takes the raw ticket and chat transcript and produces a structured summary:

"Here's a support ticket and the full chat transcript. Summarize this for an engineer in under 200 words. Include: the core problem, what we've already tried, any relevant account history, and what we need from engineering. Skip the pleasantries."

Instead of rewriting the same context from scratch every time, the agent starts with a usable draft.

The agent reviews, adjusts if needed, and sends. Engineers get what they need the first time.

Success Metric: Fewer back-and-forth clarifications on escalated tickets, faster resolution time.

Back Office: SOP Creation

Most SMBs have a documentation problem. Their processes exist, but they live only inside people's heads.

The ops team knows how to do things, but nobody has written it down. New hires figure it out by asking. When someone leaves, the knowledge goes with them.

Bonus!

Here's an AI pilot you can use to help draft new standard operating procedures. Ask the Ops lead to brain-dump a process in rough bullet points, with no structure required. Just have this person list everything they'd tell a new hire. Then they can use the prompt below to generate a shareable document:

> "I'm going to brain-dump a process we run every week. Turn it into a clean SOP with numbered steps, defining who is responsible for each step, and any tips or common mistakes. Keep it under one page."

The Ops lead reviews and publishes.

Success Metric: Number of documented processes increases significantly, and the time to produce each one drops from hours to under 30 minutes.

You don't need to redesign the whole business at once. Pick one process people already hate, then put the digital intern to work there, and learn from what happens.

PART 3

GOVERNANCE

AND SAFETY

9

LIGHTWEIGHT AI GOVERNANCE

This chapter is about building just enough structure to keep AI adoption safe without slowing it down.

When Momentum Outruns Structure

I learned this the hard way.

At BSN, momentum built faster than structure. Employees were experimenting with new tools every week, pilots were running across departments, and AI was getting wired into workflows I didn't even know about. By any measure, adoption was happening.

But I had no idea what was actually working.

Wins were real but invisible. Nobody was capturing them. Nobody was connecting the dots between what one team figured out and what another team could use.

I was the AI working group – one person trying to steer something that had grown bigger than a single person could see.

What we needed was a small group with shared visibility, a structure light enough to keep people experimenting but solid enough to capture what they were learning.

We built it eventually. The AI culture scorecard in Chapter 13 came directly out of that need. So did the working group structure here.

Both were shaped by feeling that absence firsthand.

Structure is what keeps momentum from becoming chaos.

The 2 Governance Traps

Trap 1 — Too Loose: No clear rules, people use whatever tools they want, sensitive data ends up in free accounts. That's Shadow AI.

Trap 2 — Too Tight: Security fears shut down official AI use while employees continue using personal tools in the dark. The policy says no. The behavior says otherwise.

That's Shadow AI with less visibility than before.

The sweet spot: clear guardrails that keep people and data safe, but with enough freedom that employees can still explore and improve their work.

The AI Working Group

To get started, a small AI working group is enough. There are four basic roles needed: someone from leadership, someone from HR or People Ops, someone from IT or your MSP, and someone from operations who lives in the workflows.

This group will answers questions on behalf of the organization:

- What is our AI intern allowed to do?

- What data can they access?

- How do we know it's working?

Those 3 questions sound simple. Getting the answers in writing, with everyone aligned, is the actual work.

The working group's standing mandate covers several areas:

- Approve which tools are sanctioned for company use.

- Define what data can go into which tools.

- Review active pilots and what's being learned from them.

- Review incidents or near-misses and adjust guidance accordingly.

- Maintain the AI culture scorecard.

- Update tool and data guidance quarterly or after major changes.

This team does not need to meet every week. Once the basics are in place, a short check-in every 1-3 months is usually enough.

But answering those questions is only half the job. The other half is momentum. The AI working group also keeps adoption moving, shares wins, surfaces what's working, and makes sure AI doesn't quietly fade from priority when the calendar fills up.

Someone has to own that energy. This group can provide the impetus for continued success.

What Forces the Issue

Most organizations don't build this structure because they *decided* to. They build it because a client or an auditor asked a question they *couldn't answer*.

The questions that force the issue are consistent:

- Which AI tools are your users actually using?

- Where is your data going?

- What are the retention and deletion policies on those tools?

Can you demonstrate this during a security review?

Visibility comes before policy. You can't write rules for tools you haven't found yet.

The working group's first job is the audit.

10

THE TRAFFIC LIGHT SYSTEM

I've been in a meeting with a doctor who cried over a potential HIPAA breach. Not a hypothetical one. A real conversation about what it would mean for his practice, his patients, and his career if the wrong data ended up in the wrong hands.

That's the weight behind data protection. At BSN we've spent years helping healthcare organizations understand it. We've seen what a breach costs, and not just in dollars.

When we went AI-first, that instinct sat in the back of my mind constantly. I created an AI Acceptable Use Policy early on. But I knew exactly what would happen to it.

Employees would read it once during onboarding, sign it, and never look at it again. That's how policies work. They exist to hold people accountable after something goes wrong, not to prevent the mistake in the first place.

We needed something employees could actually use in the moment. Something simple enough to remember without looking it up. Something that turned the right decision into the obvious decision.

That's where the Traffic Light System came from. Green, yellow, red. Most people already know what those mean.

The question "Is this green, yellow, or red data?" takes 3 seconds to answer and replaces a page of policy nobody has open when they need it. It's one of the most practical frameworks in this book. Use it.

Understanding Tool Types

Free or Public Tools: With individual accounts like the free version of ChatGPT or other consumer AI sites, by default, your conversations can be used to train their models. You don't control that environment.

Enterprise or Paid Tools: Tools the company pays for – like Microsoft Copilot, ChatGPT Enterprise, or business AI features in your existing platforms – typically include contractual protections that keep company data out of public model training and limit access to your organization.

The Traffic Light Rules

First classify the data. Then choose the tool.

Data Type	Free/ Public Tools	Enterprise/ Paid Tools
GREEN: Public Data (public information, generic templates, ideas that don't touch company data)	SAFE	SAFE
YELLOW: Internal Data (internal meeting notes, project plans, strategy docs, non-sensitive communications)	OFF LIMITS	SAFE (your productivity zone)
RED: Sensitive Data (customer PII, HR issues, financials, contracts, legal docs, NDAs, regulated data)	OFF LIMITS	STOP & ASK

The Simple Rules

Rule 1: In a FREE or PUBLIC tool, GREEN is the ONLY safe light. Yellow and Red are OFF LIMITS. Never paste internal work, customer data, pricing, or strategy. It's simply too risky.

Rule 2: In a PAID ENTERPRISE tool, GREEN and YELLOW are GO. This is your everyday productivity zone: internal meeting notes, project plans, strategy docs. This is where the real productivity gains happen.

Rule 3: RED is always RED, no matter the tool. Even with enterprise tools, do not paste Red data unless there is a specific, approved process for it. AI can still make mistakes, outputs can be forwarded incorrectly, and Red data needs tighter human control.

Green means go.
Yellow means use the right tool.
Red means stop.

Common Mistakes

The framework is simple. The mistakes are predictable. Here are the ones that show up most often.

- Thinking Yellow is fine in a free tool.

  It isn't. Yellow data is internal data, like meeting notes, project plans, and strategy docs.

  None of that belongs in a consumer AI account, even if it doesn't feel sensitive. The moment it leaves your environment, you've lost control of it.

- Assuming an enterprise tool makes all Red data safe.

It doesn't. Enterprise tools protect your data from being used to train public models, but they don't make Red data appropriate for AI.

Customer PII, legal documents, and regulated data still need explicit process approval before they go anywhere near an AI tool, enterprise or not.

- Not realizing that screenshots and pasted meeting notes count.

This one catches people off guard. If you screenshot an internal financial report and paste it into an AI chat, that's Yellow data going somewhere it shouldn't.

The format doesn't change the classification. The content does.

When in doubt, ask before you paste. That's the rule behind the rules.

11

TOOLS — FREE VS. ENTERPRISE

The difference between free and enterprise AI tools is not a subtle technical detail. It's the line between "this may feed a consumer AI environment you don't control" and "this is a tool your company has contracted and configured for work."

How We Got There

When we started, most BSN employees used the free versions of AI tools. That felt normal. We thought about it the same way we thought about Google Search: useful, free, and nobody asked too many questions about how it worked.

The first thing that pushed us toward paid tools was capability, not data security. The paid versions got new capabilities faster. ChatGPT Team gave us something that changed how we worked – the ability to share outputs with each other.

Suddenly AI wasn't just an individual productivity tool. It became something the team could build on together. That collaboration capability drove adoption of paid subscriptions more than anything else.

We didn't figure out the data risk on day one. We figured it out by going deeper, paying more attention, and eventually making a firm decision:

- Employees use enterprise tools for work.

- Free tools are for personal use and public information only.

That's the sequence most SMBs will follow. The goal is to get to the enterprise standard before something goes wrong.

Free and Public AI Tools

These free tools include individual accounts on platforms like ChatGPT Free, Perplexity, Claude.ai (free tier), and similar consumer-facing AI websites.

By default, conversations on free tools may be used in ways your organization does not control. Your company typically has no enterprise agreement, centralized administration, or organization-level audit trail for that usage.

Only Green data (public information) should ever touch a free AI tool.

Enterprise and Paid AI Tools

Business-grade AI tools your company pays for and controls can include Microsoft Copilot for M365, ChatGPT Enterprise, Claude for Business, Google Workspace AI features, and AI capabilities built into your CRM, support, or service platforms.

Enterprise tools typically include contractual protections that keep company data out of public model training, plus compliance certifications, centralized administration, and audit trails.

Enterprise tools make Yellow-data usage possible for everyday internal work – summarizing meetings, drafting documents, analyzing data, generating reports. That's where the real productivity gains happen.

Making the Decision

Once the data rules are clear, the tooling decision becomes much simpler.

Start with what your organization already uses. Microsoft Copilot fits naturally into M365 environments. ChatGPT Enterprise, Claude for Business, and Google Workspace AI features all offer enterprise-grade protections.

AI capabilities are also built into most CRM, support, and service platforms you're likely already paying for.

When evaluating enterprise tools, ask 3 questions beyond the feature list:

1. Does it integrate with the systems your team already uses, like M365, your CRM, or your service platform?

2. Does it support your existing security infrastructure, including single sign-on (SSO) and multi-factor authentication (MFA)?

3. Does it give IT the audit trails and access controls they need to monitor usage without blocking it?

Evaluate costs against productivity benefits, and confirm tools meet your compliance requirements before committing. Build a clear approved list and communicate which tools are sanctioned and why. Employees need to know before they can use them confidently.

Put measures in place to discourage free tools for work purposes. The goal is to make the approved path easier than the workaround.

The tools matter less than the habit of reaching for the right one.

PART 4

MEASUREMENT AND IMPROVEMENT

12

METRICS THAT MATTER

This chapter is about measurement philosophy: why you measure, what actually matters, and what to ignore.

Running on Gut Feel

For the first year at BSN, I was running on gut feel.

I knew AI was working. We'd used it to build our Microsoft 365 training curriculum and get into a market we'd never been able to reach before. But I couldn't prove it.

I couldn't quantify it, and when someone asked how AI was going, the honest answer was: I think it's going well.

That's not good enough when you're asking a company to change how it operates.

The employees who were all in on AI were easy to see. They showed up to the Friday sessions, posted in the Teams channel, and brought prompts and tools and questions. I knew exactly where they stood.

The other employees were silent, and silence could be either a good sign or a very bad one.

I had no way of knowing which. Were they using AI quietly and effectively, confused but too uncomfortable to say so, or skeptical and waiting for this "fad" to blow over?

I didn't know their comfort level, their usage patterns, or their honest feelings about what we were building.

The culture I thought we had might have been 20 people and a lot of wishful thinking.

That's when we built the AI culture scorecard.

One thing I want to be clear about is that I wasn't chasing ROI numbers. I still don't track ROI on Microsoft 365. What I know is that without those tools, my employees couldn't do their jobs.

ChatGPT and Copilot started as experiments. A year later, they were infrastructure. The scorecard was there to show us where the culture was strong, where it was fragile, and what wins we could build on. If you don't measure it, AI culture stays in the land of good intentions.

But realize that you are not measuring AI to *justify* AI. You are measuring whether the organization is becoming more capable, more confident, and safer in how it uses AI.

You don't need dozens of metrics. You need a few that actually inform decisions.

Update this scorecard once a month or once a quarter. That's plenty.

(Appendix F has a ready-to-use AI Culture Scorecard template with a completed sample.)

Leading Indicators (Early Signals)

Leading indicators show you that the work is in motion, before the results show up. The best ones tend to fall into 3 buckets.

1. Awareness & Training

Track the percentage of employees who have completed AI awareness training, and separately track those who have completed AI plus security training. Keep an eye on which departments have the highest and lowest coverage.

2. Adoption & Usage

Track how many people are regularly using your approved AI tools, and whether certain teams or roles are picking it up faster than others. Count how many AI pilots are running in a given quarter.

3. Sentiment & Confidence

Survey your team with these statements:

- "I understand how I'm expected to use AI in my role."

- "I feel confident that I can use AI safely at work."

- "I believe AI helps me do my job better."

Tracked over time, the answers will show you where confidence is building and where gaps remain.

Lagging Indicators (Results)

Lagging indicators show you whether the work paid off. These are the numbers everyone gets excited about: time saved, close rates up, support tickets down.

Rough, directional measures are usually enough at this stage. They give you proof you can actually point to.

1. Time Saved on Key Processes

How long did this process take before AI? How long does it take now? Even rough estimates are powerful: "This one AI-assisted workflow saves our team about 10-15 hours per week."

2. Quality or Throughput Improvements

Track things like the number of proposals sent per week and ticket resolution time. Compare error rates and the number of documented SOPs before and after AI assistance.

At the business level, look for faster sales cycles and higher close rates on certain deal types. Track customer satisfaction scores and backlog levels in support or operations.

Metrics to Avoid

There are easy numbers you will have access to, and they might feel sophisticated, but they don't actually help you lead.

Skip metrics like total number of AI prompts used across the company, lines of AI-generated text, or number of AI tools people have tried.

If a metric doesn't help you make a decision or improve a behavior, it's not worth tracking as a leadership metric.

13

Building Your AI Scorecard

This chapter is the operating guide for the scorecard: what goes on it, who reviews it, how often, and what decisions it drives.

What the First Scorecard Showed Us

The first time we ran our scorecard, it confirmed something I was a little afraid to see.

Half our employees hadn't completed the AI training. Half weren't using the approved tools. Half weren't actively participating in the AI culture we thought we were building.

We had a car running on 4 cylinders instead of 8.

I was surprised but not shocked. Different employees adapt at different speeds, and half the company lagging didn't mean the initiative had failed. It meant we had more work to do.

But the scorecard gave us something we hadn't had before: a clear picture of where we actually were. Not where I hoped we were, or where the enthusiastic employees made it feel like we were. Where we *actually* were.

That clarity is what made the next decisions possible. We brought the data to our leadership meetings and worked through it in the AI working group. We knew where to focus, which conversations to have, and which gaps to close first.

The scorecard showed us the gap. The gap led to a decision. The decision landed because we'd done the culture work first.

Track the Trend, Not Just the Number

A scorecard run once is a snapshot. It's useful, but limited. The real value comes from running it every month or every quarter and watching what moves.

Is training completion going up? Are more employees using approved tools? Did sentiment drop, and if so, why?

Are pilots showing results in the lagging indicators?

The trend is what tells you whether the culture is actually shifting or just holding steady. A number on its own means less than a number with a direction. That's what you're building toward.

The Scorecard Structure

Keep the structure simple.

Category	Metric	Current Status
Training & Awareness	% completed AI awareness training	[Your data]
	% completed AI + security training	[Your data]
Adoption & Usage	# of active AI pilots/workflows	[Your data]
	% using approved tools monthly	[Your data]
Sentiment	Avg score: "I understand AI expectations"	[Your data]
	Avg score: "AI helps me do my job"	[Your data]
Impact	Hours saved per week (key processes)	[Your data]

What to Do When the Numbers Are Uncomfortable

The scorecard is only useful if it changes what you do. That means knowing what action to take when it shows something you didn't want to see.

Low usage in one department usually means one of 3 things: the manager isn't modeling AI use, the team hasn't had role-specific training, or there's a trust gap nobody has addressed yet. Start with a conversation.

High training completion but low confidence means people know what AI is but don't feel safe using it. That's a psychological safety problem, not a training problem. Go back to Chapter 7.

Strong experimentation but poor process adoption means people are trying things individually but the wins aren't becoming organizational capability. That's the Individual to Organizational shift from Chapter 5. The fix is shared prompt libraries, documented workflows, and visible recognition of what's working.

The scorecard tells you where to look, but you still have to decide what to do about it.

The Quarterly Leadership Review

30 minutes, 4 agenda items.

Training & Awareness (5-10 min): Where are we? Any departments behind on required training?

Adoption & Pilots (10 min): Which teams are using AI regularly? Any new pilots started or completed? What worked? What didn't?

Sentiment & Safety (5-10 min): Are people more confident? Any issues surfaced around data or misuse? Did we learn from them?

Impact & Next Focus (5-10 min): 1 or 2 concrete wins to celebrate. 1 or 2 areas to target for the next quarter.

If the scorecard isn't changing decisions, it's just reporting.

You've got the metrics. Next up is Part 5, which gives you the 90-day plan to move them. Three phases, 12 weeks, and a clear sequence from alignment to results.

PART 5

YOUR

90-DAY

ACTION PLAN

"Strategy without execution is just theory."

14

Phase 1 — Align & Announce (Weeks 1-4)

What Phase 1 Actually Feels Like

We were among the earliest SMBs to go AI-first. There was no roadmap, no case studies written for companies our size, no one ahead of us to follow.

We made our own path. This book is the guide we didn't have.

Phase 1 doesn't feel like a clean checklist. It feels like uncertainty with a direction.

When I started pushing BSN to become an AI-first company, the questions came quickly. We were a cybersecurity company. Employees had joined to build something in that world.

Now all I talked about was AI.

Some concerns were raised directly. Others came back through managers. What was crystal clear in my head was foggy to the people I was asking to follow me.

That gap is normal. It's not a sign that your team doesn't trust you or that the direction is wrong. It's what happens when a leader envisions something the organization hasn't seen yet.

Your job in Phase 1 isn't to eliminate the uncertainty. It's to give people enough structure and enough reassurance to take the first steps anyway.

The goal of the first 30 days is momentum, not transformation: a few people experimenting, a few wins shared, and a message clear enough that employees stop filling in the blanks with their own worst assumptions.

Start there.

Goal: Get aligned at the top and send a clear, reassuring message to the organization.

Who's involved: Leadership, HR, IT/MSP, and one or two ops leaders.

Key Actions

1. Form Your AI Working Group

3-5 people: leadership, HR, IT/MSP, ops. Align on a shared commitment of responsibility for guiding AI tools, guardrails, and learning.

(Appendix C has a Working Group Charter template with defined roles and meeting cadence.)

2. Write Your AI Story in Plain Language

Share why you're using AI, the framework of AI as a "digital intern," and your commitment to training and oversight. This will become the backbone for all-staff emails, town halls, manager talking points, and your "AI at Our Company" one-pager.

3. Decide Your Initial Approved Tools

Pick one or a small set of tools people can safely use for work. Make it explicit that your chosen tools should be used for work, and that personal accounts should not.

4. Create or Update Your "AI at Our Company" One-Pager

Include your AI story and the digital intern framing, approved tools clearly labeled as enterprise vs. not approved for work,

Green/Yellow/Red data guidance, and what to do if you're unsure or make a mistake.

(Appendix D has a fully written sample one-pager you can adapt. Appendix B has the master 90-Day Plan Template to fill out with your working group.)

5. Launch Internal Communication

Leadership sends an all-staff message. HR posts the one-pager where people can find it. Managers are given 2-3 talking points to use in team meetings.

6. Enroll All Employees in AI Awareness Training

Within the first month, enroll every employee in baseline AI awareness training covering AI basics and limitations, Shadow AI risks, the digital intern concept, and the Green/Yellow/Red data classification model. Make it time-bound to be completed within the next 2-3 weeks.

Month 1 Outcomes

By the end of the first month, you should have a leadership group steering the ship, a clear story replacing silence and rumors, basic guardrails and tooling in place, and every employee on the same page through AI awareness training.

That's the foundation. Everything in Phase 2 builds on it.

15

PHASE 2 — PILOT & LEARN (WEEKS 5-8)

How to Run Pilots People Actually Follow

Our pilots at BSN weren't clean. We didn't have this book or any roadmap. We had curiosity, a direction, and a willingness to try things and share what happened.

The culture we built around the pilots is what made them work.

From the start, I told the team: "We're experimenting together. We're learning together. Nobody has all the answers, including me."

That framing gave everyone permission to try things, get things wrong, and keep going. It turned out to be the most important thing I said.

I also made a decision early on that every win would be amplified. Every single one. When something worked, I shouted it from the rooftops, including company meetings, LinkedIn posts, and calls with our MSP partners.

The drumbeat of AI success did something a memo never could. It made people believe this was real and it was working.

Our Friday sessions started small. A handful of curious employees shared what they were trying, what was working, and which new tools were worth looking at.

I didn't set them up to build culture. I set them up to share information. But that's exactly what they became. Every week more people showed up. People who weren't directly involved in any pilot started attending because they didn't want to miss what was happening.

A pilot doesn't have to *involve* everyone to *belong* to everyone. Five people may be running the experiment, but if the whole company is following along, hearing what worked and what didn't, and seeing wins celebrated and failures treated as learning, then the whole company is part of it.

The culture shifts even for the people who never touched the tool.

We followed those sessions with a Microsoft Teams channel for sharing prompts, discoveries, and wins. The channel gave the energy from the sessions somewhere to live between Fridays.

Goal: Prove value and learn from real AI pilots in a few key processes.

Who's involved: Ops leaders, frontline teams, AI working group, HR for training support.

Key Actions

1. Pick 2-3 Pilot Processes

Use the pilot selection criteria from Chapter 8: digital and text-heavy, repetitive and frequent, easy to check, annoying but important. Examples: sales follow-up emails, support ticket summaries, SOP drafting, internal meeting summaries.

(Appendix E has the full Pilot Selection Checklist with a completed example.)

2. Design the AI-Assisted Workflow for Each Pilot

Map 4-6 steps. Decide where the AI intern helps (draft, summarize, structure). Write 1-2 standard prompts per process.

Clarify that humans *always* review and approve.

3. Enable the Pilot Teams

Assemble a small group of people who actually do the work. Give them access to approved tools, quick role-specific training, and a clear reminder of data guardrails.

4. Run the Pilots for 30-45 Days

Ask teams to track rough time before vs. after AI, examples where AI helped, and examples where AI failed or needed heavy editing.

5. Start Filling in Your Scorecard

Start capturing early signals in the scorecard:

- training completion for pilot teams
- usage and adoption
- rough estimates of time saved or quality improved

Weeks 5-8 Focus

The goal is learning. Put the AI intern into a real job and see what happens.

16

PHASE 3 — SCALE & EMBED (WEEKS 9-12)

The People Who Were Already There

Here's something that took 3 years to fully understand.

For the first 2 years of BSN's AI transformation, we didn't automate a single process: no n8n, no Claude Code, no agentic workflows.

What we did was simpler. We gave employees access to ChatGPT and Microsoft Copilot, trained them, gave them guardrails, and got out of the way.

That alone produced the gains described in Chapter 1, which included productivity improvements, new revenue streams, and the cultural shift. All of it came from people using tools, not from technical automation infrastructure.

The automation came later, and it came from an unexpected place.

One of our salespeople kept showing up differently. He was reading AI newsletters, following developers on X, experimenting on his own time, and bringing what he found back to the team.

He and I traded discoveries constantly. Neither of us had formal training or a roadmap. We were just curious, and we had a culture that rewarded that curiosity.

Over time he kept picking up more skills. Eventually I moved him out of sales and into a new AI automation group we built specifically because of what he'd become.

He wasn't a programmer when he started. He's not the profile most companies would have hired into an AI role. He was a salesperson who leaned in when most others were still waiting to be told what to do.

You don't have to hire for AI skills. The people who will build your AI capability are probably already on your payroll. You just have to build the culture where they can emerge.

Scale comes from noticing who's leaning in.

Once our automation team was up and running, departments didn't come to them asking for AI workflows. They came with problems they'd been tolerating for years.

Marketing made a change in HubSpot that triggered a sync of 15,000 records into Salesforce. The sync updated existing records. Marketing and sales pointed fingers at each other.

Nobody had a way to reverse it. Weeks of manual cleanup stretched out in front of the team.

The automation group used n8n to identify every record the sync had touched and roll back the changes. It took only a few hours. The relief in the room was visible.

That was AI automation in a form most people don't picture. No machine learning, no generative output. Just a team with tools powerful enough to do in hours what would have taken weeks by hand.

This team is now 4 people and growing, built not from a hiring plan but from a culture where someone could grow into a function because the business discovered it needed them.

Goal: Share what you learned, make some changes stick, and prepare for the next 90 days.

Who's involved: Leadership, HR, ops, AI working group.

Key Actions

1. Review Pilot Results

For each pilot, document what worked well, what didn't, roughly how much time it saved, and whether it improved quality or throughput.

Decide to *Scale* (make it the new standard), *Tweak* (adjust prompts and steps and try again), or *Drop* (document why and move on).

2. Capture 2-3 Concrete Success Stories

"Support used AI to summarize ticket histories. Result: 20% faster escalations, fewer back-and-forth questions."

"Ops used AI to draft SOPs. Result: 4x more processes documented this quarter."

Turn these into short internal case studies or slides.

(Appendix G has a Success Story Slide template with fill-in fields designed for all-hands sharing.)

3. Share Wins Company-Wide

Leadership highlights AI wins in an all-hands meeting or newsletter. HR or ops invites pilot team members to share how they did it and what they learned. This builds momentum and reduces fear.

4. Formalize Your One-Pager and Scorecard

Update your "AI at Our Company" one-pager based on what you learned. Populate your AI culture scorecard with training data, adoption and pilot data, and a few lagging metrics like time saved and quality improvements.

5. Decide Your Next 2-3 Priorities

Which roles or departments to focus AI training on, which new processes to pilot, and any governance updates needed on tools, data guidance, or oversight.

End of Week 12

By the end of Week 12, AI should feel less like a scary unknown and more like a normal tool: real wins on the board, a scorecard tracking progress, and a clear plan for what comes next.

What Success Looks Like After 90 Days

Day 0	Day 90
No clear message about AI	A clear AI story everyone has heard: "AI is our digital intern"
Employees guessing or hiding usage	Employees know approved tools and guardrails
No agreed tools or guardrails	At least one approved enterprise tool and Traffic Light System in place
No examples of AI helping	2-3 documented AI pilots with tangible wins
No metrics beyond "turned on a tool"	Simple AI culture scorecard reviewed regularly

Is everything done? No. But you've moved from "We should probably do something about AI" to "Here's exactly what we're doing, and here's how we know it's working."

That is what scale looks like in an SMB: not complexity for its own sake, but instead you'll amplify visible wins, shared capability, and a clearer next move.

CONCLUSION

THE LEADER'S CHOICE

By the time most SMB leaders finish reading this, they fall into 1 of 2 camps.

The first group puts the book down with good intentions. The calendar fills up. The urgency fades. AI adoption gets pushed to next quarter. Shadow AI keeps spreading. The competitive gap keeps widening. Nothing changes. They understood the problem. They just didn't make the decision.

The second group schedules a meeting.

What You're Actually Deciding

Your people have already made their own AI decision. 75% of them are using it right now, in free accounts, without guardrails, outside your visibility. Some of those choices are harmless.

Some may be moving client data into public AI environments you don't control. You can't tell which.

Leadership silence on AI sends a message. Your team reads it as permission to hide their usage, to guess at what's acceptable, or to look for a company that's figured this out. That's the real cost of inaction: not always a breach or a lawsuit, but a slow drift that compounds month over month until you're far behind where you could have been.

The decision has already moved past "should we adopt AI?" The question is whether you'll shape what that looks like, or inherit whatever version develops on its own.

Three years after going AI-first, BSN has employees raising their hands asking to automate their own jobs. We have a workforce that finds AI applications without being told to, and tools that are deeper and more ambitious than anything we had in year one.

A single year of culture-first work got us there. The technology actually followed. It was the people who led.

What It Actually Takes

None of that required a genius plan. It required a decision, followed by consistent effort over time, and a clear story that people could hear and act on.

A small group owned the momentum. A handful of real pilots proved the value. A scorecard showed where we were making progress and where we weren't.

This book gives you the blueprint.

Start with the first phase. Learn from it. Build from there.

Your Next Step

In the next 2 weeks, schedule a 60-90 minute working session with your leadership team, HR, ops, and your MSP. Form your AI working group. Pick your first 2-3 pilot processes.

Set a date for your first culture scorecard review.

Once those are on the calendar, the plan is real.

You've read the book. Your employees are already using AI. The only question left is whether *you* lead it or *it* leads you.

APPENDICES

APPENDIX A

THE 90-DAY ROADMAP AT A GLANCE

Everything in this book leads here. This appendix collects every template, checklist, and scorecard from the 90-day plan into one place. Fill them out, in order, with your working group and you'll have a real program, not just a good intention.

Your Complete Resource Suite

Resource	What It Does
90-Day Plan Template	The master operating document. Filled out by Leadership, HR, Ops, and IT.
AI Working Group Charter	Establishes ownership and governance for the steering committee.
"AI at Our Company" One-Pager	The employee-facing policy and guardrails document.
Internal Comms Kit	Announces the plan and the "Digital Intern" story to the full team.
Pilot Selection Checklist	Picks the right processes for Phase 2 pilots.
AI Culture Scorecard	Tracks training completion, adoption, and business impact.
Success Story Slide	Scales wins and builds momentum in Phase 3.

The 3 Phases

Phase 1: Align & Announce (Weeks 1-4)

Goal: Get aligned at the top and send a clear, reassuring message to the organization.

- Form the AI Working Group (Leadership, HR, Ops, IT) to guide tools and guardrails.
- Define the "AI Story" (AI as a "Digital Intern," not a replacement).
- Select initial Approved Tools and establish data safety rules (Green/Yellow/Red).
- Launch Internal Communications via leadership email and manager talking points.
- Roll out Baseline AI Awareness Training to establish the mindset and safety rules.

Phase 2: Pilot & Learn (Weeks 5-8)

Goal: Prove value and learn from real AI pilots in a few key processes.

- Select 2-3 Pilot Processes that are text-heavy, repetitive, and low-risk.
- Design Workflows by mapping steps and identifying where the AI "intern" assists.
- Enable Teams with tool access, micro-training, and specific prompts.
- Run Pilots (30-45 days) while tracking time savings and quality.

Phase 3: Scale & Embed (Weeks 9-12)

Goal: Share what you learned, make changes stick, and plan the next 90 days.

- Review Results to decide whether to Scale, Tweak, or Drop each pilot.

- Capture and Share Success Stories company-wide to build momentum.

- Formalize the AI Culture Scorecard to track training and adoption long-term.

- Plan the Next Priorities for the next 90-day cycle.

APPENDIX B

THE ONE-PAGE 90-DAY PLAN TEMPLATE

This is the document that makes the plan real. Fill it out during your first working group session, not after, not later. A plan that lives only in someone's head isn't a plan. Build it on paper with names and dates attached.

Company Name:____

Date:____

I. Strategic Goals (The "Why")

Identify the top 3 goals for the next 90 days (e.g., "Make AI expectations clear," "Run 3 pilots," "Establish governance").

1. ____

2. ____

3. ____

II. AI Working Group (The Owners)

Name	Role / Department	Responsibility

III. The 90-Day Roadmap

Use the Phase 1, 2, and 3 checklists in Appendix A as your action items here.

IV. Pilot Processes

Focus on text-heavy, repetitive, low-risk tasks.

Process Name	Owner	Team	Success Metric

V. Key Communications Schedule

When	What
Week 2-3	All-staff announcement from Leadership
Week 4	"AI at Our Company" One-Pager posted and distributed
Weeks 9-12	Pilot updates and "Win" stories shared company-wide

Sample: Completed 90-Day Plan

Below is an example of how a completed plan looks.
Use it as a reference when filling out your own.

Company Name: Apex Innovations, Inc.

Date: October 1, 2025

Strategic Goals:

1. **Establish Safety & Governance**: Eliminate shadow AI usage by formally rolling out the "Traffic Light" data policy and getting 100% of staff through baseline AI Awareness Training by Week 4.
2. **Prove Value via Pilots**: Launch and complete 2 targeted pilots (Customer Support Ticket Summarization and Marketing Content Drafting) to validate a minimum of 20% time savings per task by Week 8.
3. **Build the "Digital Intern" Culture**: Shift the internal narrative from fear to empowerment by publishing 3 verified Success Stories and setting up the permanent AI Working Group.

Sample AI Working Group

Name	Role / Department	Responsibility
Sarah Jenkins	Executive Sponsor (COO)	Set the story and tone; approve strategic priorities; publicly celebrate wins to drive culture.
David Ross	HR / People Ops (Director of HR)	Build AI policy into employee onboarding; coordinate "AI Awareness" training assignments; enforce guardrails.
Elena Rodriguez	Operations	Select the specific pilot processes; design the new "AI-assisted" workflows; track time savings and quality metrics.
Mark Alston	IT / MSP (TechSecure MSP)	Decide approved tools; maintain Green/Yellow/Red data guide; monitor technical security.

Sample Pilot Processes

Process Name	Owner	Team	Success Metric
Support Ticket Summaries	Jordan Lee (CS Manager)	Customer Support	Reduce average time-to-understand history from 15 mins to 3 mins per ticket.
Marketing Content Drafting	Priya Patel (Marketing Lead)	Marketing	Increase content output by 50% (3 posts/week to 4.5) without extra hours.
Client Meeting Recaps	Michael Chen (Acct. Director)	Sales / Account Mgmt	Send detailed follow-up emails with action items within 30 minutes of meeting end.

Appendix C

AI Working Group Charter

The working group needs a charter for the same reason a pilot needs a flight plan. Everyone needs to know who owns what before something goes wrong. This template takes 20 minutes to fill out and removes weeks of ambiguity.

Core Responsibilities

Governance	Policy	Oversight
Decide approved vs. prohibited AI tools.	Maintain the Green/Yellow/Red data safety guidelines.	Review the "AI Culture Scorecard" (training and adoption).

Meeting Cadence: Bi-weekly during the first 90 days. Monthly after that.

Charter Template

Company: ____

Effective Date:____

I. Mission Statement

To steer the organization's adoption of AI, making sure it's used safely, effectively, and in alignment with company values. We guide the culture, training, and guardrails to turn AI from an external threat into a trusted "Digital Intern."

II. Core Responsibilities

(List the specific governance, policy, and oversight duties assigned to this group.)

III. Decision-Making Authority

(Define what this group can approve, escalate, or veto.)

IV. Meeting Cadence

First 90 Days (Implementation): Bi-weekly

Ongoing (Maintenance): Monthly

APPENDIX D

"AI AT OUR COMPANY" ONE-PAGER

This is the document your employees actually read. Not the policy memo, not the all-hands slide deck – this brief overview. Keep it to one letter-sized page. Put it somewhere people can find it on a Tuesday afternoon when they're not sure if it's okay to paste something. The sample below is a starting point. Rewrite it in your company's voice before you publish it.

Sample One-Pager

Effective Date: October 1, 2025

1. The Philosophy: Your New "Digital Intern"

We're adopting AI to handle the repetitive work (drafting, summarizing, organizing) so you can focus on the high-value work that requires your judgment, creativity, and relationships.

The Mindset: Treat AI like a smart, eager, but inexperienced summer intern.

The Rule: It can do the heavy lifting, but you verify everything. You're the manager; the AI is the assistant. Never copy-paste without reading.

2. The Toolbox: What Can I Use?

We only use enterprise-grade tools that don't train on our data.

APPROVED (Safe to Use)	PROHIBITED (Do Not Use)
Microsoft Copilot (logged in with work email)	Free ChatGPT / Claude (personal accounts)

APPROVED (Safe to Use)	PROHIBITED (Do Not Use)
ChatGPT Enterprise (Work Space)	Any "PDF Summarizer" found on Google
Adobe Firefly (for images)	Grammarly Free (browser extension)

3. The Traffic Light System: Data Safety

GREEN: GO (Open Business Data). Safe to share freely in approved tools.

- **Public information**: marketing copy, website text, industry news.
- **General logic**: brainstorming, coding help, Excel formulas.
- **Routine content**: drafting emails, summarizing public articles, meeting agendas.

YELLOW: CAUTION (Confidential Business Data). Safe ONLY in our Enterprise Workspace. Never in free tools.

- **Internal IP**: strategic plans, internal memos, SOPs.
- **Client data**: contracts, project specs, meeting transcripts.

  Requirement: Make sure you're logged into your Work Account. If the chat window says "Personal" or "Free," this data is off-limits.

RED: STOP (Toxic Data). This data creates legal or security liabilities and is never appropriate for the AI.

- **Strict PII (Identity)**: Social Security Numbers, Driver's Licenses, Medical Records.
- **Access Credentials**: passwords, API keys, MFA codes, admin logins.
- **Sensitive Financials**: unmasked credit card numbers or bank routing numbers.

4. The Golden Rule

"You are the Pilot." AI's suggestions are not facts. If the AI hallucinates a statistic or writes a biased email, you're responsible for the final output. *Read it. Tweak it. Own it.*

Questions? Contact the AI Working Group at [email address].

APPENDIX E

PILOT SELECTION CHECKLIST

Picking the wrong pilot is the most common Phase 2 mistake. Teams choose something ambitious or visible instead of something that's actually a good fit for AI assistance. This checklist takes the guesswork out of it. Run every candidate process through both tests before you commit.

Part 1: The "Sweet Spot" Test (Must Answer YES to All)

If you answer "No" to any of these,
this process probably isn't a good fit for a first pilot.

Criteria	Yes / No	Notes
1. Is it text or data heavy? (Does it involve reading, summarizing, or drafting?)		
2. Is it repetitive? (Does this happen often enough to matter?)		
3. Is there a "Human Guardrail"? (Is there an expert who will review the output before it's final?)		
4. Is the data "Safe"? (Can this be done without using "Red" toxic data like passwords/SSNs?)		

If you answer "Yes" to any of these, stop.
The risk is too high for a first pilot.

Risk Factor	Yes / No	Notes
1. Does it require 100% accuracy without review? (e.g., auto-sending emails or unverified financial calculations)		
2. Does it require recent physical-world knowledge? (e.g., breaking news from 5 minutes ago)		
3. Does it involve "Red" Toxic Data? (SSNs, passwords, health records)		

Part 3: The Decision

[ ] APPROVED (Proceed to Pilot)

[ ] REJECTED (Too risky / Not enough ROI)

Pilot Goal:

Tool:

Sample: Completed Pilot Selection Checklist

Process Candidate: Monthly Client Status Reports

Proposed By: Client Success Team

Part 1: The "Sweet Spot" Test

Criteria	Yes / No	Notes
1. Is it text or data heavy?	YES	Requires reading 4 weeks of email updates + CRM notes.
2. Is it repetitive?	YES	Happens 50 times/month (once per client). Takes 45 mins each.
3. Is there a "Human Guardrail"?	YES	The Account Manager must review/edit before sending to client.
4. Is the data "Safe"?	YES	Uses client project updates (Yellow Data), safe in our Enterprise tool.

Part 2: The "Red Flag" Test

Risk Factor	Yes / No	Notes
1. Does it require 100% accuracy without review?	NO	It's a draft. Human review is mandatory.
2. Does it require recent physical-world knowledge?	NO	Relies only on the provided internal notes.
3. Does it involve "Red" Toxic Data?	NO	Strictly project status updates.

APPROVED (Proceed to Pilot)

Pilot Goal: Reduce drafting time from 45 mins to 10 mins per report.

Tool: ChatGPT Enterprise (Data Analysis feature).

APPENDIX F

AI CULTURE SCORECARD

A scorecard you look at once is a snapshot. A scorecard you look at every month becomes a compass. The scorecard template below tracks the 3 things that actually tell you whether your AI culture is moving: training readiness, real adoption, and business impact. Fill in your baseline numbers first. Everything else is just watching the direction.

I. Talent & Training Metrics (Are We Ready?)

Metric	Goal	Actual	Trend	Status
Baseline Training Completion (% of all staff who finished "AI Awareness" training)				
Weekly Active Users (% of staff logging into Enterprise Workspace)				
Shadow IT Detection (attempts to access blocked free tools)				

II. Pilot Performance (Is It Working?)

Pilot Name	Success Metric	Current Result	Status

III. Risk & Sentiment (How Does It Feel?)

Metric	Insight

IV. "Win" of the Month

Win Title: ____

Winner's Name: ____

Description of the Win: ___________________________________

Next Review Date: ____

Sample: Completed AI Culture Scorecard

Company: Apex Innovations, Inc.

Period: Month 2 (November 2025)

Status: ON TRACK

I. Readiness & Adoption

Metric	Goal	Actual	Trend	Status
Training Completion (% who finished "AI Awareness")	100%	94%	+10%	On Track
Weekly Active Users (% logging into Enterprise Workspace)	50%	68%	+15%	On Track
Shadow IT Detection (blocked free tool attempts)	< 5	3	-2	On Track

II. Pilot Performance

Pilot Name	Success Metric	Current Result	Status
Support Ticket Summaries	Reduce review time to < 5 mins	4.2 mins (down from 15)	On Track
Marketing Content	Increase output by 50%	+35% (still ramping up)	In Progress
Client Recaps	Send within 30 mins	20 mins (avg)	On Track

III. Risk & Sentiment

Metric	Insight
Employee Sentiment	72% say "AI helps me do my job better" (Survey). Sales team is most enthusiastic; Admin team is hesitant.
Safety Incidents	1 Near Miss: User pasted a password into the chat but deleted it immediately. Action: Resent "Red Data" reminder to team.

IV. "Win" of the Month

"The Proposal Hero"

Sarah in Sales used the Data Analysis feature to digest 3 years of spreadsheets for a client review. What usually takes her 4 hours of Excel work was done in 20 minutes. She used the extra time to refine the pitch strategy.

Next Review: December 5, 2026

APPENDIX G

SUCCESS STORY SLIDE TEMPLATE

Wins that don't get shared don't spread. This template gives you a repeatable format for capturing what worked, who did it, and what changed. Use it in all-hands meetings, internal newsletters, or your Teams channel. One good story, told clearly, does more for adoption than another training session.

For each success story you capture, fill in the template below.

AI WIN OF THE MONTH

Who: [Name, Role]

The Task: [What were they doing?]

Before AI: [How long did it take? What was the pain?]

After AI: [How long does it take now? What improved?]

In Their Words: "[Direct quote from employee about experience.]"

Example Format

"Support used AI to summarize ticket histories. Result: 20% faster escalations, fewer back-and-forth questions."

"Ops used AI to draft SOPs. Result: 4x more processes documented this quarter."

Turn these into short internal case studies or slides. The format doesn't need to be fancy. It needs to be specific enough that someone in a different department can see themselves doing something similar.

About Breach Secure Now

BSN was built on a simple observation: the technology people need most is usually the technology they're least equipped to navigate on their own.

Art Gross started Entegration in 2000, bringing IT services to small and midsize businesses during the internet's early years. In 2009, as HIPAA regulations tightened, he built HIPAA Secure Now to help small healthcare organizations get compliant before the enforcement wave hit. In 2015, with ransomware attacks accelerating and small businesses bearing the brunt, he launched Breach Secure Now to bring security awareness training to the companies that needed it most but had no way to find it.

Today BSN trains more than 1 million employees across 35,000+ businesses. The training reaches those businesses through a network of Managed Service Providers, the IT companies already serving SMBs as their outsourced technology partner.

BSN goes to market exclusively through MSPs. They deliver the program, support the rollout, and stay involved as the culture develops. BSN uses that same MSP-led model to help SMBs adopt AI safely and practically.

For organizations that want help implementing this approach, BSN and its MSP partners offer an AI Risk to Adoption program built around executive alignment, risk assessment, a 90-day roadmap, and ongoing training.

The frameworks, tools, and templates in this book reflect the same approach BSN uses in the field. The appendices are a working version of that, built to be filled out, not filed away.

If you already work with an MSP, ask them how they are helping clients address AI governance and adoption. If you don't currently have one, you can find a BSN partner at breachsecurenow.com/contact-us-smallmedium-form/#contactus-section.

ART GROSS is a serial entrepreneur and the CEO of Breach Secure Now, a leading provider of human-centric cybersecurity, AI awareness, and HIPAA compliance training for Managed Service Providers (MSPs). Known for building mission-driven companies with strong, people-first cultures, Art has spent over four decades at the intersection of technology, security, and healthcare.

He began his career as a Corporate Systems Architect at Merck & Co., Inc., and in 2000 founded Entegration, Inc., which he continues to lead today. Entegration provides IT services to healthcare organizations, including some of the largest fertility practices in the world.

In 2010, Art launched Breach Secure Now to help MSPs address the human side of cybersecurity and manage HIPAA compliance. In 2024, the company expanded its mission to include productivity training, introducing Microsoft 365 and AI awareness programs to help employees work more securely and effectively.

He also founded HIPAA Secure Now to help medical practices comply with HIPAA regulations and protect patient information, and Inskyber to provide cyber insurance solutions for MSPs and their clients.

Art holds a B.S. in Computer Science from Penn State University and an MBA in Management from Fairleigh Dickinson University. His leadership continues to shape how MSPs build trust, strengthen security, and help businesses become more productive in today's complex technology environment.